The Orkney Yole

The Fisherman By Robert Rendall

Aald Jeems o' Quoys, wha erst wi' leid and line
Keen as a whitemaa, reaped the Rousay Soond,
And in his weathered yawl a twalmonth syne
Set lapster-creels the Westness craigs aroond,
Nae stroke o' fortune cloured wi' bluidy claa,
Nor glow'ring daith wi' sudden tempest mocked
But in his wee thatched croft he wore awa'
E'en as a cruisie flickers oot unslockt.
Nae kinsman raised, nor wife, nor weeping w'ain,
But we, his yamils, this memorial stane.

The above is reproduced with permission from the estate of Robert Rendall and the following is reproduced with permission from the literary executor of George Mackay Brown, Brian Murray.

Boat and Croft by George Mackay Brown

The Skarf nearly did for Scad.
Fitting thwarts
Rob got a nail in his thumb. He died in the croft
Bunged to the eyes with rust and penicillin.
One night when Burra Sound was meltings of silver
Under the moon, and the uncles of Scad with wands
Enchanted cuithe and sillock, she dipped a bow.
She ushered Tam, his pipe still in his teeth
To the hall of cold green angels. They hauled her up
Among the rocks, in the track of Angus of Scad
Whose neck fluent with drink from the cattle mart,
Snapped like a barley stalk. Quarry-dragged then,
An outcast tree with tins old boots smashed bottles
She warped, in a bed of seedless stone, a winter.

Ignorant, sweet, in stardark, from swiftstorm, a tryst,
A throb among barren curves.
The opening sky. Fissures. A drift of seapinks.
Seaward, the herring in shoals.
(Is summoned from unborn hosts one hungerer).
The Skarf was uprooted.
She was probed, fireblown, patched, puttied, painted.

A boy climbed with his haddocks
(And half turned back) to Scad, and a new cold cry,
And (from old looms) unfolded, the fold of light.

Ward, "keeper of plows". That name they gave him.

c.1886, at 8.6M probably the largest three sailed yole built in Orkney, to ferry lighthouse keepers and supplies to the Pentland Skerries from Burwick. Thomas Budge, NLB, helming.

Foreword

"Oh, for a Swiss army knife!" Sometimes you have a small job to do, such as cutting a line or changing a plug or getting a stone out of a horse's hoof and if you only had such a thing in your pocket, all would be well. It is the original multi-tool, and a bye-word for adaptability and problem solving. Such is the mystique of this little red knife from Switzerland that we often compare other things favourably with it: the Land Rover, the DC3 Dakota aircraft, the Grey Fergie tractor. All have been called the Swiss army knife of their field.

Why? Because not only are they excellent at the job for which they were designed, rugged, reliable and dependable; they have also proved their worth by taking on almost any job you throw at them. Adaptable, useful, hard-working and, ultimately, much loved and inevitably iconic.

So, in the Orkney yole, I give you the Swiss army knife of the seas! (You knew this ramble had to be going somewhere!) Ostensibly a fishing boat, and a very good one. Perfectly suited, through a long process of evolution, to its home waters. Its two masted rig clears a space for sorting the catch, its wide stable hull rides over the swells and chops of narrow island tideways and brings the fisherman back home. The yole, it turned out, had so much more to give; so many blades hidden in its handle!

Sunday excursions, regatta sailing, taking island produce and even livestock to market. Flitting, bringing the doctor and evading the press gang. The Orkney yole provided these services and so much more besides. Perhaps summed up by the name of one well-known yole: *Family Pride*, these boats really were treasures to their owners and communities' lifelines and livelihoods.

I hope you enjoy this book; I feel privileged to be asked to contribute to it. In these pages there is something for everyone, stories, anecdotes, pictures, facts, figures and information from a range of contributors. Thanks must go to the members of the Orkney Yole Association and others who have made this book possible with their knowledge, memories and efforts.

So, turn the page, I give you – the Swiss army knife of the seas: the Orkney yole!

Mark Shiner

The Nav School, Stromness

2008 sail on the OYA yole Lily just after launching, crewed by our younger sailors. This South Isles yole was built by Ian Richardson using Lottery Grant funding.

2014 South isles yoles Helga and Solwen sailing close hauled in Stromness harbour. Both yoles were built by Ian Richardson.

THANK YOU

A heartfelt thank you to all who have helped to make this Orkney yole book a reality. Included in no particular order are: -

SPONSORS

- Scapa Whisky
- Scottish Sea Farms
- Stromness Community Council
- EMEC

We could not have produced this local book without your local support.

CONTRIBUTORS

- All the folk credited on each article who, with or without any arm twisting, have freely and enthusiastically written articles, given interviews and given permissions to reprint old articles. We couldn't have done it without all your effort and work.

- All the folk who provided photographs, drawings and information which were essential to this book. A special mention for David Mackie of the Orkney Library and Archive, who scanned many old yole prints in the past five winters for the book. Individual photographs are credited at the back of the book.

ORKNEY YOLE ASSOCIATION ("OYA")

- All the Editing Sub Committee for their enthusiasm and long hours adjusting articles and re-writing some of my work into English. Chair: Caroline Butterfield; Ron Bulmer; Thorfinn Johnston; Maurice Davidson.

- All the OYA Committee members who have supported this book over the last three years, including the above Editorial Team members and Jan Andersen, Willie Tulloch, Ian Richardson and Ken Sutherland.

iDesign for providing an efficient and cost-effective local Orkney publishing service, and putting up with complete beginners at book production.

And my wife Debbie, for endlessly helping an I.T. dinosaur to write on a computer.

And most of all a huge thank you to YOU for buying our yole book, with all the proceeds going towards the Orkney Yole Association and our work in promoting the future and preserving the past for all Orkney's old, traditional boats.

This first ever book on Orkney yoles is a small spark of hope for a bright future, to emerge from this grey Covid 2020 year.

Maurice Davidson, Commodore, ORKNEY YOLE ASSOCIATION

1936 photo of Swona and Stroma yoles in Swona's sheltered Haven. Sale of the wreck SS Croma attracted them. K101 is the Star of Burwick, WK529, front right, is now the Hope.

In memory of Allie Kirkpatrick, and all past Yole sailors

Allie Kirkpatrick sailed yoles in Longhope when he was a lad, changed to yachts in Kirkwall in midlife and came back to yoles when the OYA was formed in 2000. He was always keen to share his wealth of experience and skill with everyone, especially young folk. He also came out to name and inform all the old photos we had of yoles at our dark winter evenings at Flaas Pier. And never missed out on the maintenance, cleaning and painting of the OYA yole Lily, which he adopted for eight years.

But the activity he enjoyed the most was racing yoles in all wer isles regattas in the summer months. Racing in close competition with up to nine of our yoles against his OYA Lily. Quiet, determined and a good observer, with sixty years of experience and skill, he usually came in first over the line, with a smile on his face. And he had a good dram and a yarn with his crew after the trophies were dished oot. Energetic to the last, enthusiastic always and a kindly but determined man to ken. He died early in 2019 and is missed by all of us.

Yoles and this Yole Book are only possible due to all the efforts and skill of past yole sailors. A generation ago they were mostly all poor crofters quietly heading out on cold and rough days to feed their hungry families. Some did not return and have no memorial. To the memory of these silent yole sailors, mainly forgotten now and with no graves, we write this book as our memorial to you. You are not forgotten. Thank you. MD

Commodore OYA 2020

Allie Kirkpatrick at the tiller of his favourite Yole Lily during the Holm Regatta 2014, with crews of Lily and Sumato behind.

Early 1900s photo of the herring Zulus drifting out of Stromness harbour with locally built fishing yoles moored off the stone piers.

Contents

		Page
	Foreword	iv
	Thank you	vi
Introduction		1
Section 1	**History and development of the Orkney Yole**	
	Origins by Maurice Davidson	5
	Lineage of the Orkney Yole by Sheena Taylor	13
	The Orkney Yole – a brief history by Dennis Davidson	21
	Local development of Yoles in and around Orkney by Maurice Davidson	29
	Yole oars, sails and engine by Maurice Davidson	41
	The Ness Yole and the Orkney Yawl – two northern types of boats by Arthur Johnston	45
	Stroma and Swona Yoles by Maurice Davidson	49
	Praams and flatties by Maurice Davidson	55
	UNESCO Intangible Cultural Heritage, the Kysten Forbundet and the Orkney Yole Association by Ron Bulmer	57
	Yole, yoal or yawl? Give the yawl a smakk by Ron Bulmer	63
Section 2	**Yole uses**	
	Yoles for fishing by Maurice Davidson	71
	Other uses for Yoles by Maurice Davidson	83
Section 3	**Recollections of life with yoles**	
	Salutary tales from Hoy – as told by John Budge	91
	Hoy Sound Meets Terry – Terry Thompson tells a tale to Ron Bulmer	95
	Memories of Hoy - Sailing Experiences of Fifty Years ago by G.L. Thomson	101
	A Graemsay Crofter. Some of Frank Davidson's memories from 1917 onwards	107
	Orkney Yoles in Harness by Sheena Taylor	109

Section 4	**Learning to sail**	
	Yole Spik by Maurice Davidson	119
	The sea and how I got into sailing by Captain Willie Tulloch	131
Section 5	**Regattas**	
	Extract from "The Man on my Back" by Eric Linklater	141
	2017 regatta reports by Sheena Taylor	145
	Windy Westray by Maurice Davidson	153
Section 6	**Building and restoring Orkney Yoles**	
	Building an 18-foot South Isles Orkney Yole by Ian B Richardson	163
	Building the *Lily* by Sheena Taylor	173
	Ian Richardson's boatbuilding career – interview by Maurice Davidson	175
	The restoration of the *Sumato* by Captain Ken Sutherland	183
Section 7	**Out at sea on a Yole**	
	A day at the Auld Man by Maurice Davidson	191
	A sail roond Hoy by Maurice Davidson	197
	Rock and Roll round South Ronaldsay 2013 by Maurice Davidson	201
	Referendum sails round Eday by Maurice Davidson	205
	2011, Small Ships and Tall Ships by Maurice Davidson	209
	Mowatt Family Yoles – *Hope, Star of Burwick* and *Vivid* by Sheena Taylor	211
	Willie Mowatt's stormy sail to the Skerries 14 June 1959 by Maurice Davidson	215
Appendix	Development of yoles to the south and west of Orkney by Maurice Davidson	223
Register of Yoles in seaworthy condition		226
Glossary		228
Further reading		230
Photograph credits		231
References		232

Introduction

The Orkney yole is a wooden, clinker-built, double-ended open traditional sailing boat native to Orkney. It is a beamy (wide) vessel, making it buoyant and able to carry substantial cargo. They were built locally following Norse boat-building traditions as a seaworthy workhorse in the days before inter-island ferries became the norm. Yoles were used for all the day to day trips that the farmers and fishermen of the islands made when needing to fish or travel or transport goods and livestock.

In the 20th century the yole almost died out, as passenger and vehicular ferries allowed inter-island transport in greater comfort, speed and safety. The few that remained were neglected and often in a poor condition, with the wooden hulls being left to rot in barns and on beaches in the unforgiving Orkney climate.

In December 2000 a group of enthusiasts formed the Orkney Yole Association (OYA) with the aim of preserving the craft and promoting its use. The association's members comprise a small nucleus of owners, active sailors and supporters who want to preserve this once vital part of the economic and social life of the islands. From only one traditional yole regularly sailing, we now have ten new and restored yoles active in Longhope and Stromness. We also have our own new South Isles yole *Lily* with her traditional flattie tender, and meet and sail from our restored sail house at the end of the old stone Flaws' pier next to the Stromness museum.

The OYA is a self-financing charity, relying on funds generated by its members' efforts. All profits from this book will go towards the association's work. New members are always welcome and our skippers enjoy having visitors out with us.

This book is a celebration of the Orkney yole. It has been compiled by members of the OYA and contains both contemporary and historical photographs of the various types of yole that have been sailed over the years. There are also chapters explaining their history, evolution and construction, together with first hand reminiscences from sailors of these unique vessels.

Section 1 charts their Norse lineage, with Maurice Davidson noting clinker building traditions in places as far away as Borneo and China, and speculating on how the technology may have travelled from Syria to Scandinavia, and then on to Orkney. His brother Dennis details their development in Orkney from the 1660s and Sheena Taylor gives insights drawn from Norwegian burial finds, replica boats and place names in Orkney. Maurice adds further articles on specific developments of the yole within Orkney and Shetland, and complemented by a fascinating article published in Yachting World in 1936. Ron Bulmer ends with two articles indicating a commonality of design with boats still afloat along southern Scandinavian coastlines and highlighting how the name yole has travelled not just from Scandinavia but on through France and beyond.

Section 2 covers the varied uses of the yole through articles from Maurice. This theme is expanded on in Section 3, with a number of tales from a variety of sources from Hoy, and Sheena's insights from tales told by her father and grandfather.

The South Isles yole Helga sailing with the strong Burra Sound tide to Hoy and round Graemsay on one of our fine Covid 2020 summer days. Flood tide out and ebb tide back to Stromness.

Section 4 has two very different articles on learning to sail: one from Maurice and another from Captain Willie Tulloch, while section 5 takes us into the exciting world of regatta sailing – including a description from Eric Linklater, an exhilarating and evocative piece.

Section 6 opens the window on what it is like to build and restore a yole. Ian Richardson shares a fund of knowledge from an entire career in boat building and in a later article tells how he got into that career and is responsible for Orkney yoles being scattered across the whole of Europe. Sheena describes the journey to build the OYA's own boat, the *Lily*. And Captain Ken Sutherland tells us how a few beers led him into restoring a 100-year-old yole and how, after 25 years in the Merchant Navy, he finally learnt to sail.

The final section contains a selection of articles from Maurice in his Orkney dialect describing expeditions in his yole all around our isles. The section concludes with the editors' favourite: Willie Mowatt's amazing tale of how he and his crew survived stormy conditions in the Pentland Firth on a trip in his yole, the *Hope*, from John O'Groats to Burwick, when they were blown east to take shelter in the Pentland Skerries. Sheena has documented some of the Mowatt family of yoles in the preceding article and gives us a taste of the challenges they faced in their local waters.

Views expressed in each article are those of the individual author and not necessarily shared by the OYA.

So, friend, turn the pages, enjoy the photographs, be stimulated by the articles. And thank you for supporting this wonderful boat.

The OYA 2021 Round the Flow cruise, involving four yoles and a small yacht, found this hidden gem, St. Vincent's jetty on Flotta.

Stromness fishermen Willie Budge and Willie Thompson c.1890 tarring the inside of their three sailed yole Mary Jane at Graham Place slip. Stern heightened and forward thaft rope worn.

Section 1 History and development of the Orkney Yole

*[**Editors' note:** Maurice Davidson, in this first article, describes how the Orkney yole is descended from clinker-built boats brought to Britain by the Norse and speculates how the Norse boat building technology may have travelled to Scandinavia from the Middle East with the help of Phoenician traders. He notes how clinker boats were independently developed in China and other parts of the world where wooded rivers met the sea. Later articles explore how the Norse boats were adapted to meet local needs in these isles and eventually became what we today recognize as the Orkney yole. This is not intended to be an academic treatise, but rather to give a broad overview with insights gained from Maurice's overseas travels and trips on replica boats.]*

ORIGINS by Maurice Davidson

Most folk agree that yols, jolles, yoals (terms used across Scandinavia) - or yoles as we call these boats in Orkney - came to Britain with the Viking raiders, refugees and then traders from Bergen and Stavanger in Norway, from 800A.D. onwards. These yoles were narrow, with sharp, curved ends, and shallow, made from just three or four wide pine planks, or strakes, clinched together with tree nails, then soft iron rivets along their edges, set on a few oak frames. Such clinker built yoles were light and fast to row in the tideless Norwegian fiords, which are sheltered behind their chain of islands. They were new to us Britons, who were used to heavy carvel river barges, log boats and hide coracles.[i]

A stiff timber backbone keel was also new to most river-type barges around at the time. Keels strengthen the hull over sea swells and against waves, help to keep a straight course when rowing or sailing, and protect the thin strakes from rocks at sea and scrapes when hauling up the shore every day. River boats need none of these features.

Yoles were sea boats for fishing and travel, not lazy barges for slowly carrying heavy cargo, drifting down a river. With splayed V sections fore and aft, they cut through the water easily, whilst having a more rounded middle for holding cargo and people. With removable seats or 'thafts' (thwarts), these four or five metre long yoles could be easily stacked for transport on larger longships. Small yoles could be used for rowing folk out to larger moored ships, or for fishing and transport for two or four folk at most, as they were quite narrow, being only one metre or so wide. Oselvar yoles from Hardanger, Norway, still show all these traditional features.[ii]

Norse traders brought their clinker yoles over to Orkney, stacked on deck or flat-packed for ease of construction, so IKEA flat-packs are nothing new. The traders sold them to farmers, to fish part-time off Orkney's shores for cod and saithe. These were favoured fish in Norway, as they are easily air-dried in salt spray, on the shoreface.[iii]

The Norse found an abundance of fish round Orkney, especially next to tide rips, which exist only in the north of Norway.

Willie Tulloch's small and narrow Hardanger faering from Norway, rowing and sailing at Portsoy annual Traditional Boat Festival, 2006. She was the smallest boat there, with unique sail design.

Salt fish became the staple food of Orcadians for winter, along with fresh cuithes[1] and codling, in huge inshore shoals during summers. With regular and abundant high-energy food for all, farms could be developed, land dug and drained and sillocks (tiny fish once plentiful inshore) used by the ton for fertiliser, even until 90 years ago.

These early, small, imported Norway yoles changed everything, suddenly giving easy access to our inshore seas for many. Lack of trees here was overcome by these invaders, carrying timber with them to trade. Life was no longer just a scramble for shellfish among the ebb, or the odd fish trapped in loch or shore.

Norway has all the trees needed to make boats, the Norse cutting, splitting and smoothing light and oily larch or spruce with their axes, those long and narrow blades of iron. (Iron ore is found in huge heaps on the hills of the north of Norway.) Vikings made their axes infamous with their formidable terror campaigns, before settling down as landowners and wealthy traders. They travelled all the way down the coasts of the UK and Ireland to found their major trading posts in Dublin and York, connected to the sea on large rivers.

Records from Bergen show the king of Norway welcoming Orkney and Shetland traders in 1186. In the early 1500s records still show seven large trading boats from Norway carrying 17 yoles to Shetland, 12 to Orkney for cod fishing, two to Leith and 700 flatpack yole strakes to Orkney and Shetland, with 1,500 to Leith one year.[iv]

But how did the Scandinavians develop their new clinker yoles and longships and how did they do it so quickly? Boatbuilding there can be traced back to the early iron age with the Hjortspring boat discovery in Southern Denmark, and had evolved to the graceful Nydam boat, by 300A.D. or so, this being their earliest known clinker-built boat.

Almost all of the rest of Europe constructed carvel-built boats, these having heavy frames with heavy planks pinned to them, and the gaps between caulked with oakum. These were easier to build and repair than clinker-built boats, but were much heavier, hard to steer and slow in use.

Poor and isolated, Norway had only fish, some furs and timber to trade, which generated little surplus funds to develop new boat technology, or to provide fine ironwork for axes and rivets.

But other developments were happening in the Baltic, just to the east of Norway. And these new traders from the east seemed to carry huge amounts of silver and gold from the Middle East[v].

Recent university research from Croatia and Turkey shows that iron clinker rivets have been found all along the Northern and Eastern shores of the Mediterranean.[vi]

---

[1] coalfish, Pollachius virens, from one to three years old

Norway and Sweden still sail their spreet (sprit) sailed yols. The yols are wide like the South isles yoles, to help sail the boats level, and shallow as they sail in sheltered fiords.

These date from Roman times onwards, and were mainly used by Phoenicians, who were major traders from Syria, employed by Greeks and Romans to supply goods and ships.[vi]

Phoenicians left Syria in their boats and sailed all over the then-known world, to the shores where iron rivets have been found from this era, 1,800 years ago. And like many refugees, they took everything: their family, money, technology and skills with them, to start up anew.

These wealthy foreign shipping traders were not particularly welcome, so had to keep moving on. They travelled to Rome, Turkey and up major rivers from the Black Sea, as researched by BBC4 history series on Viking burials in 2016. Many eventually settled in remote and safe ports in the East Baltic, like Kaliningrad in Lithuania and Riga in Latvia, where Middle Eastern communities still live. Both of these ports are served by major rivers from the south.

Here they met up with the trading Vikings. Huge buried hauls, including thousands of mainly silver dirham coins from Iraq and Tashkent, have recently been found in Gotland, the island freeport of the Baltic. Silver would have been traded for fish and fur.

More Viking remains and burials have been found in Russia than in all other lands put together. So maybe the East was their main trading route, rather than the West. St. Petersburg's hinterland rivers in Russia still have Viking-style rowing yoles, just like the modern Shetland Ness yoles. There's nothing new under the sun!

With these Eastern traders came their light, easily carried, smaller, clinker, double-ended boats. Could this have been a source of the Vikings' new clinker technology? This must be a possibility. An awful lot of other inventions have come in from the East, in fields such as mathematics, astronomy and even religion. So why not the humble clinker boat?

It appears that the Chinese also built clinker boats, sharp ended river craft found in the muddy banks from the later part of the 7th century onwards.

In Borneo, six to ten metre long, hollowed-out log boats were standard on all the rivers, when I lived there in the early 2000s. But near the coast, Arab/Malay trading tribes pegged wide boards of wood overlapping the log edges, raising the sides to carry more fish and making the boat more seaworthy. These were double ended, timber, clinker boats.

So maybe everywhere wooded rivers flow into the sea, all over the world, folk developed clinker boats to meet their needs, in such an obvious and simple way?

Vikings developed light, shallow clinker boats to a high point with their graceful 20 metre longships. From recent Norse Boat research in Scandinavia, clinker double ended timber boats were built all over the North of Europe. Finnish oral yole records indicate that designs came from Turkey and Arabia. Falbåts preserved from the 1500s look like narrow, Ness or Fair Isle yoles, with high bows to rise over the ice for seal hunting. The names of the boat parts are the same as for yoles here in Orkney. Deeper sharp sterns were also developed for sailing, just as here.[vii]

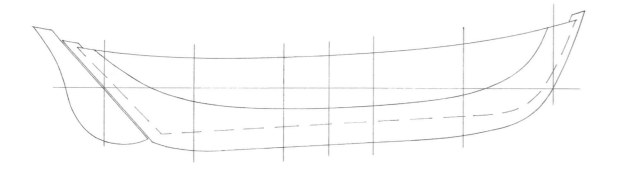
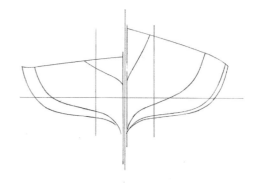

*Hull Lines of South Isles Yole - "Emma"
Built by J Nicolson, Flotta, 1912*

LOA 18', Beam 7'

Measured and drawn by D C Davidson

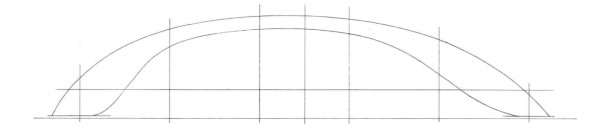

Hull section, plan and elevation of the South Isles yole Emma, built in 1912 by J Nicholson, well known boatbuilder in Flotta, for fishing and lobster. Many yoles were built in Flotta.

The rig of Sami and old Swedish yoles looks more like that of dhows from Arabia, with their lateen-looking lugsails[vii]. The Sami live in the far north of Scandinavia, fishing and herding reindeer, living a very hard life. Their clinker Kalajoki boats were built between seven metres and sixteen metres long, with a curved stem to gently ease boats onto ice or beaches, and a straight sternpost for a rudder, just like here.

Smaller Gnovttesissat, at five metres long, again look like sharp, narrow Fair Isle yoles, with names of boat parts similar. Interestingly, in some areas running the boats and fishing was entrusted to the Sami women. [vii]

So, the humble Orkney yole has a fascinating ancestry and may well be closely linked to technology travelling from Turkey and Arabia through northern Scandinavia and coming across with the Vikings. This resonates with similar developments of clinker boats in many other parts of the world.

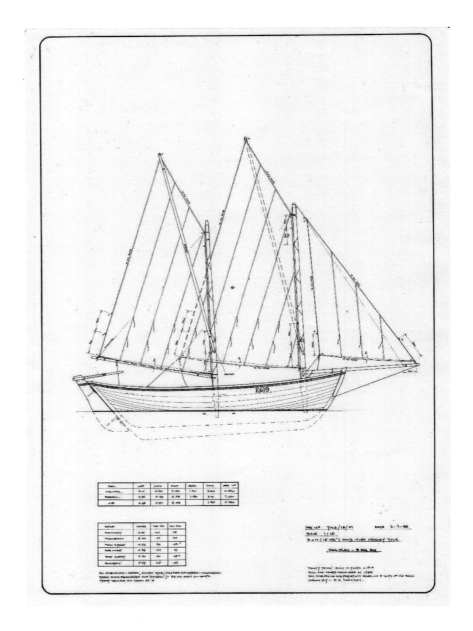

Opposite: Elevation of the South Isles yole Family Pride, built in Flotta c1910 for the Kirkpatrick family who still own and sailed her until recently. Drawn by Dennis Davidson.

Over a hundred folk at the sunny OYA harbour sail day and BBQ at our pier, 2019. Fifty three folk went out sailing in four South Isles yoles -- Lily, Helga, Waterwitch and Gremsa.

[This next article by Sheena Taylor presents a very different perspective from that of Maurice Davidson, building our picture of Norse influence. Sheena introduces us to the yole's shared characteristics with Norse boats dating back to the 8th and 9th centuries, although we never expect our yoles to reach the 17 knots of the Sea Stallion that Sheena sailed alongside. And she tells how place names in Orkney give clues as to the types of Norse boats traversing these isles.]

LINEAGE OF THE ORKNEY YOLE by Sheena Taylor

The modest, clinker-built yoles in Orkney today owe much to Norse influences in design, as described and illustrated elsewhere in this book. The use made of yoles as fishing, cargo and transport vessels links them to the knǫrr, or knarr, and to other smaller vessels used in settlement of new areas, rather than to the raiding longships in what has come to be known as the 'Viking' era, so glamourised by Hollywood film productions.

Nevertheless, both the older vessels and the ones we use today share characteristics displayed in the long, elegant and well-preserved Oseberg ship, found in 1903 and excavated from a burial mound near Tønsberg in Vestfold on Outer Oslofjord the following year.

Beautifully decorated with interlaced beast carvings on the prow and ornate spiral stem heads, the Oseberg ship dates from around 800 A.D.. That boat may never have gone to sea, and is thought to have been built as a ceremonial burial ship. When first unearthed, although it had been plundered, the ship contained the remains of two ladies, at least one of whom was high-ranking, still accompanied by goods to use in the afterlife.

The Gokstad ship, dating from around 850 A.D., found a little further south in 1880, more closely matches the archetypal image of Norse longships – the long, shallow-draft vessels, which carried raiders to wreak terror on coastal areas round Scotland, England and Ireland from the end of the 8th century until the middle of the 11th century. The Gokstad ship was also excavated from a burial mound – a 'hauge', like howe, as in Maeshowe, and Hoxa.

The ship contained the remains of what is described as a tall, well-built man. The horses, dogs, smaller boats, a sledge and tents, harnesses and other riding gear he would need in the afterlife throw light on his status and activities, when alive, as does the peacock also found there. More valuable precious metal goods are thought to have been removed during early plunder of the mound.

The oak hull, with pine decking measured around 76 feet in length, beam of 17 feet drawing 6½ feet, was secured by iron rivets, unlike earlier vessels, which had used more flexible fastenings of the strakes. The ship is thought to be capable of warfare and of transporting people and cargo.

Although the vessel was well preserved in clay, its restoration was not completed until 1930. The Oseberg and Gokstad ships are both displayed in the Viking Ship Museum at Bygdøy in Oslo.

An exact replica of the Gokstad ship was constructed by 1893 by the Norwegian sea captain, Magnus Andersen, named *Viking*, and sailed across the Atlantic to attend Chicago's World Fair, where the ship still remains.

Sheena Taylor aboard the Havhingsten. Note the steering oar and pulley system to Sheena's right.

He recorded a spell between 15th and 16th May when the vessel covered 273 nautical miles; was surprised to report the ship's performance sailing to windward to be comparable to the 'modern' two-masted vessels he was more familiar with; praised the flexibility of the hull because of the method of lashing planks to the ribs, especially in heavy seas or facing head-seas and marvelled that they could make headway, when well reefed in gale conditions.

The steering oar mounted on the starboard aft quarter of these vessels, which gave the name 'starboard' to that side of all vessels, gained his most effusive praise, much preferring the side rudder to a stern-post rudder, never 'kicking' as a stern post would be expected to do. One man could steer using merely one line to help.

He clearly enjoyed his voyage and wrote:

"In the semi darkness the light from the northern horizon cast a fantastic pale sheen on the ocean as *Viking*, light as a gull, glided over the wave tops."[viii]

The voyage of the replica oak-built ship, named *Havhingsten fra Glendalough* (*Sea Stallion from Glendalough*), which visited Orkney en route from Roskilde in Denmark to Dublin in 2007, also illustrates the speed and range of these vessels. The original boat, completed according to some records around 1042 A.D., with length 96 feet, beam 12 feet and drawing only 3 feet, is the second longest longship to be discovered.

I was welcomed aboard the ship in Kirkwall harbour and given a guided tour of both the traditional features of the vessel and the modern navigation and safety equipment. The steering oar, I noted, was rigged with a block and tackle to make life easier for the helmsman. Perhaps the greater length of the *Havhingsten* compared to Viking longships made that necessary. Nor were they relying on a lodestone compass and word of mouth advice for navigation, with modern charts and electronic navigation aids aboard.

I also had the good fortune to be on our own sailing boat visiting Inverie, just north of Mallaig, when the *Havhingsten* arrived there. Local people were ready to receive the crew, which had to row for a considerable part of that leg of their journey when wind fell away. When they did arrive in the small hours, they were greeted at the pier by a noisy, 'armed' reception party in kilts with faces painted blue, as if daubed in woad. More helpfully, that group had transported the gear brought earlier by the expedition's support boat and set up the crew's tents for them.

The following day some people I had met in Kirkwall spoke of being disappointed by calm seas rounding Cape Wrath. The most testing conditions of the whole voyage were ahead of them in the Irish Sea – posing a challenge they and the boat handled well.

When the visit to Inverie of a day or so was over, the *Havhingsten* and the accompanying support boat left the pier, just as we too dropped our mooring, the tides being most favourable and a forecast of strong winds to follow by nightfall.

For a while we sailed from the bay alongside *Havhingsten*, until oars were shipped and the large, square sail was fully raised in more open water.

Havhingsten leaving Kirkwall, 19 July 2007.

As we negotiated the tricky entrance to the safe haven at Arisaig, the *Sea Stallion* galloped off 'at a rate of knots' – around 17 knots, it was later reported – towards mist over distant Ardnamurchan point, to appear from the haze in Tobermory ahead of schedule.

What terror would have been generated, when a ship of that sort emerged out of the mists to come ashore near Wicklow, south of Dublin, its crew rushing inland towards the land-locked water of Glendalough. Those raids were repeatedly inflicted on that locality and others like it, not only for the rich pickings to be had from the undefended religious settlement there, but for the timber from which the original *Havhingsten* would be built and launched for use on further violent raids.

Hermann Pålsson, my teacher of five and a half decades ago, and his friend and collaborator in Norse Studies, Magnus Magnusson, both used the term 'viking' as a verb. To go 'a-viking' was to set off in the summer months to raid and plunder, but also to find useful resources for future use, lucrative trading opportunities and, crucially, to locate suitable areas for settlement. They conjectured that the word, perhaps, suggested penetrating bays in other countries, going into a 'vík' on an unknown coast for shelter from the sea and to extract lucrative plunder from the inhabitants.

Some sailors made that activity a way of life, but others went a-viking for a year or two in their youth before settling to earn their living as farmers, tradesmen or craftsmen. [Not quite the 'gap year' fashionable among young adults nowadays.]

When areas for settlement were identified, different types of vessel came into play. The knǫrr, or knarr, shorter than the longship at around 54 feet, and beamier, around 15 feet, was built to carry a number of people and all kinds of cargo, weighing as much as 24 tons on ocean travel. That could include animals - horses, farm animals and poultry – and materials for building a house, as well as household goods, such as furniture and smaller goods and chattels to set up a new home.

New Norse settlements were thus established to the west of Orkney and Shetland and the Hebrides, first to the Faeroes and Iceland and from there, onwards to Greenland and Newfoundland. Over a thousand years ago, as told in the sagas, settlers from L'Anse aux Meadows, Newfoundland, travelled onward to 'Vinland' in modern-day North America, settling there, at least, for a time.

These boats may also have carried goods eastwards for trade in the Baltic and less frequently to Spain and the Mediterranean. River craft travelled as far as the Caspian Sea, and onwards by land to meet international caravan trade routes.

The Book of Settlements, the Landnámabók, recording the settlements in Iceland between 874 and 930, describes how the settler would cast his high seat pillars (part of his furniture) overboard, intending to make his home where they came ashore. Their fate, and his, would be decided by the Gods….and the nature of the currents along the coast.

Among other evidence, recent research suggests that the place-name, Knarston, situated well inland on Orkney's mainland near Dounby, may indicate a stopping place for cargo-carrying boats, so as to avoid long and hazardous sailing journeys in more open waters.[ix]

Daniell print c.1820. Fishing yoles off Wick harbour with old square sails, from the Viking days.
Orkney changed to easier-tacked lug and spreet (sprit) sails at this date.

Smaller boats – the karve, or karfi, the færing (originally with four oars) and several other types of small craft - were used in inland waters. It is from that stable that the reliable, capable yoles - the seafaring work horses of the islands – descend.

Harald, the Fair-Haired, (according to the sagas but now under dispute) initiated the unification of the small kingdoms in Norway into one kingdom in 872 A.D., a process not completed until the first half of the 11th century, around the time Christianity was adopted.

Orkney was subject to the Norwegian and Danish crowns with the Norse Jarls competing for power in the islands until 1468, when Orkney and Shetland were ceded to James III of Scotland in payment of a previously agreed marriage settlement.

Under the Scottish crown came the era of Scottish Earls, which saw King James VI installing his half-uncle Robert Stewart as Earl in 1581.

The source of power over the whole of Scotland shifted further south with the Union of the Crowns in 1603 linking Scotland to England and Wales under one sovereign. The Treaty of Union - the Union of the Parliaments in 1707 – further consolidated that shift, as did the defeat of the Jacobite Rebellion in the 1740s.

What has survived in Orkney through the centuries of Norse and later seafaring societies?

In general terms the remnants of Orkney Norn, a form of Norse spoken in the islands, is still evident in some communities. With a significant separate vocabulary, word order and grammar from English, that form of speaking qualifies as a language, rather than simply a dialect. Vocabulary and terms connected with the sea and boating are part of that heritage. Perhaps that language accompanies a unique, difficult to define, outlook on life. (A topic for another day!)

In specific terms, traditional boat-building skills have been passed on and developed, usually by the apprenticeship method – things like selecting materials, identifying the correct bend in timber for a well-shaped, sturdy prow, the use of specialist methods and tools like steaming, bending and clamping 'straiks'. If no longer wielding an adze, the special knack, artisan skills and, most importantly, pride in painstaking craftsmanship has been handed on.

There were many more boat-builders at one time in Orkney than we have now, rendering those still engaged in the activity the more valued.

In addition, as demonstrated in this book, the ability to handle these small boats in challenging northern waters was also passed on by the mariners of yesteryear.

Most importantly, in Orkney, we still have a number of yoles to sail in a wonderfully inspiring area of water around our islands.

The OYA three sailed Yole Lily was successfully sailed by these three young trainees in the breezy Stromness Regatta 2021. Orkney yoles are well suited for our tidal seas.

[Dennis Davidson, elder brother to Maurice, has spent his career as a naval architect. His scholarly article charts historical records of boats in Orkney from the mid-17th century. There he describes their many uses throughout the isles and the introduction of the sprit-sail rig, which can still be seen on the Gremsa (owned by Maurice Davidson) and the OYA's Lily. He also notes the differences in boats between the North and the South Isles, reflecting the different influences coming up from the south and down from the north.]

THE ORKNEY YOLE – a brief history by Dennis Davidson

Surviving records do not disclose when the first Orkney yole was built. However, documents describe how its larger cousin, the 'great boat' or 'big boat' was built in Orkney from as early as 1662.[x] It is likely that smaller boats would also have been built at this time. With few trees growing on the islands, timber to repair and build boats had to be imported or salvaged from shipwrecks and re-worked. Jettisoned cargoes of timber and ocean driftwood were also used.

While some boats were being built in Orkney, they were also imported from Norway throughout the eighteenth and early nineteenth centuries. Four-oared and six-oared boats were occasionally shipped over, often un-assembled 'in boards', being more compact to stow in the holds of small Orkney trading vessels. Island carpenters would then assemble and fasten the boat parts together. Between 1787 and 1796, more than 200 boats were imported from Norway to Orkney.[xi]

In 1750, a 'yole' equipped with four oars, a rudder and a single mast with yard was built in Shapinsay.[xii] While no dimensions for the boat are stated, the large quantity of deals (pine boards) used for planking together with the loads later carried by the boat suggest that this was a much bigger boat than the slender four-oared boats imported from Norway. The yole was often hired by Kirkwall residents to transport boat-loads of peats from the North Isles to the town. We also know of two boats being built in Stromness in 1759.[xiii]

Around 1782, Captain MacLeod of Rodel in Harris on the Outer Hebrides hired the services of 'some East Country fishers, with Orkney yawls', to teach the inhabitants fishing techniques.[xiv] This is the earliest known use of the term 'Orkney yawl' or yole, suggesting it was by this time a boat-type known outwith the islands.

In 1790, Stromness merchant David Geddes encouraged Thomas Balfour (Shapinsay) to participate in the herring fishery, using two or three good Orkney boats of 18 foot with good sails according to the burden of his vessel to fish with nets.[xv]

Daniell print of Stromness harbour, c1820, with Orkney yoles hauled up the North End beach. Also a narrower yol imported from Norway. Many pilots for shipping used yoles.

While Dutch deep-sea herring fishermen set and hauled their nets from the decks of their busses[2], Scottish herring busses employed three boats with nets for the fishing process. The buss provided a floating base for the 18 fishermen and their catch as well as a means of travelling to and from the fishing grounds.

Rev. George Low reported in c.1795 that eighteen boats with keel lengths between 16 and 17½ feet were used by the fishermen of Birsay for inshore fishing from four summer stations. Their boats were built by Stromness carpenters and cost 2 shillings per foot of keel, a fully equipped boat with fishing tackle costing on average about £10 Scots.[xvi] These were probably six-oared boats manned by the 144 fishermen living in Birsay at this time.

During the latter half of the eighteenth century more than 300 sailing ships called at Stromness and Longhope each year.[xvii] Since wars with the French rendered the English Channel passage too risky because of roaming privateers, many ships sailed north-about. Local Orkney fishermen and ship masters, particularly at Stromness and Longhope, found new employment as pilots for visiting ships.[xviii] Their pilot boats were probably big yoles, perhaps painted regulation black and rigged with two masts and sprit-sails when making a longer passage out west, down Scapa Flow or to meet a sail approaching in the Pentland Firth. While the publication of Murdoch MacKenzie's charts of Orkney (1750) provided shipmasters with details of safe channels and tidal streams around the islands, licensed pilots and their boat crews continued to find employment at Stromness and Longhope for more than 100 years.

In 1816, Samuel Laing encouraged the establishment of a herring station at Whitehall village in Stronsay. After a slow start, the venture blossomed and by 1822 there were 186 local boats and 28 larger vessels fishing from Stronsay in summer.[xix] After several successful seasons, as many as 400 North Isles boats, many of them small open yoles, were being fitted out for the herring fishing.

As local fishermen became more successful, a need for bigger, faster boats arose, so that the night's catch could be landed fresh for gutting each morning. Boatbuilders in Stromness started building what were essentially big yoles later called Orkney herring-yawls. By 1883, however, James Omond was writing of the 'discarded Orkney herring-yawl' with 20 to 30 feet of keel 'peculiar to the Orkneys' which had been 'supplanted by the firthy and the smack rig.'[xx]

Yoles from Rackwick and Walls in Hoy, Burwick and Windwick in South Ronaldsay and Swona had long been used to fish for cod and ling in the Pentland Firth and for lobsters around the island shores. Before creels were introduced in c.1850, two men in a small yole fished for lobsters using rings with baited nets. Captured lobsters were stored in kists[3] afloat, before being despatched south to the Thames alive in well-smacks, and later by rail to the fish market in London, where they were in great demand by the gentry.

---

[2] A herring buss, a Dutch fishing vessel, decked with two masts and used to fish for herring offshore.

[3] Lapster kist, a perforated wooden box or chest for holding live lobsters afloat until sent to market.

Stanley Cursiter's iconic painting in the Stromness Museum, of Linklater and Greig's large Baikie's yole motoring in to their sheltered Yesnaby noust, 1920s.

In 1786, nearly 40,000 cod were caught by Walls fishermen and delivered to the fish-house on the Aith where the catch was cured. The fishermen were paid two pence for each cod and the laird Major Moodie of Melsetter claimed his fish teind[4] in cash.[xxi] Twelve yoles each with six men on board were launched into the Pentland Firth at Skippi Geo, near Brims, to fish with handlines when sea conditions allowed.[xxii]

It is unclear when the sprit-sail rig was first tried on South Isles yoles. Samuel Laing suggests the rig was introduced by visiting lobster smacks from England in the late 1700s.[xxiii] A Flotta pilot boat which capsized in breaking seas off Swona in 1847 was rigged with sprit-sails and by 1880 the rig was commonly seen on yoles all around Scapa Flow, extending as far north as Birsay and east to Holm including all the South Isles.[xxiv] The sprit-sail rig was also used on small yoles at Stroma and Caithness. By 1830, North Isles yoles had abandoned the single square-sail in favour of a two-masted lugsail rig, which allowed boats to sail closer to the wind.

In 1880 John Tudor, while visiting Orkney and gathering information for his book *The Orkneys and Shetland; Their Past and Present State*, noted a considerable cod and ling fishery was being carried out by open boats from the North Isles. He reported that the smaller boats throughout the South Isles were sprit-rigged and built on the same lines as boats in the south, while the North Isles boats approximated more to the Shetland yawl and were generally smack or cutter-rigged. It is unclear which North Isles boats he referred to.

Throughout the latter half of the eighteenth and early nineteenth centuries, the manufacture of kelp[5] from seaweed brought much wealth to Orkney lairds and merchants. Boats with nets were used to gather tangles and ware[6] from the skerries and in 1798 Thomas Balfour's estate included two large boats for gathering tang[7].[xxv] These were probably large, flat-bottomed yoles used with oars.

Later, when affordable, coal was shipped regularly from Newcastle, crofters from Graemsay loaded their yole with bags of coal at Sutherland's Pier in Stromness and sailed across Hoy Sound.[xxvi]

Graemsay yoles were also used to transport bolls[8] of grain to the mill at Cairston, Ireland (Stenness), or sometimes Hoy, for grinding. Then, when tractors replaced the horse and ox in the early twentieth century, barrels of fuel had to be transported to the island. Ten sheep might be carried over to the town market while larger animals such as cows and horses were usually transported on bigger, sturdier boats such as the *Ark*, a big North Isles yole originally built for the Commissioners of Northern Lighthouses in c.1850.[xxvii]

---

[4] One tenth of the produce, in this case fish caught and landed.
[5] Kelp was formed by burning tangles (type of seaweed) in kilns (pits) and the solid cake produced was shipped south and used by glass and soap manufacturers who required potassium salts.
[6] Different types of seaweed

[7] A generic name for large, coarse seaweed growing above low-water mark
[8] A dry measure, a boll of meal amounts to 140 lb. avoirdupois (Scottish National Dictionary)

Quoy's small South Isles yole (wider quill for sailing), Mary, anchored out of the Hoy Sound tide waiting for slackwater to sail to Stromness from Graemsay.

Before the paddle steamer *Royal Mail* started to deliver mails across the Pentland Firth in 1856, mails were transported from Burwick in South Ronaldsay and Huna in Caithness on two four-oared boats, which met mid-firth and transferred mail sacks and any brave passengers in what must have been a hazardous operation in a swell.[xxviii] Yoles and skiffs transported mail to and from all the inhabited islands to the mainland of Orkney. Similar open boats ferried passengers on request between Scarfskerry in Caithness and Walls in Hoy, landing below Snelsetter or on the beach at Brims.

By the end of the nineteenth century, boatbuilders were to be found building and repairing yoles, skiffs and dinghies on many of the Orkney islands with distinct differences arising between the North and South Isles boats. With the ebb and flow of boatbuilding work, all but a few town-based boatbuilders still worked a croft or went to the fishing to eke out a living. The Flotta yole was refined by Nicholson, the Westray skiff by Reid and Miller, the Sanday yole by Scott and Omand, and Baikie in Stromness built many sailing yoles, including a few fitted with motors for fishermen in Stromness, Graemsay, Hoy, Caithness, and Sutherland.

Many fishermen fitted motors in their sailing yoles after about 1909.[xxix] The sailing ballast together with sails and spars were left ashore and some yoles had an extra strake fitted together with side decks to allow for the stern squatting when under power.

As we have seen, yoles were essential for the island communities of Orkney to survive up until about the 1970s, when ro-ro ferries were introduced to serve most of the inhabited islands. Yoles were used by crofter-fishermen to transport peats and later fuel, grain and weekly messages (provisions), mails, small animals, and passengers, including the doctor and those attending the kirk on nearby islands. Yoles were used to catch fish for the table, lobsters for cash to pay the rent and take part in the occasional whale hunt when whales strayed into island bays. Island fishermen and creel-men used yoles and skiffs to catch fish and lobsters using lines and creels and for more than 100 years the pilots of Stromness and Longhope used yoles to board sailing ships seeking a pilot. Also, prior to the establishment of lifeboat stations around the islands, yoles were often launched in response to sailors in distress as well as for the plundering of some shipwrecks.

By the end of the twentieth century, only a few traditional yoles were still being launched and sailed for pleasure in the summer months. The two-masted rig had been replaced by a single mast with gunter mainsail and jib, which was handier for competitive sailing in the local regattas. The refurbishment of a small Flotta yole and the *Family Pride* together with the building of two new yoles by Ian Richardson and Len Wilson in the late 1990s resulted in a resurgence of interest in the Orkney yole for recreational sailing, which was further stimulated by the formation of the Orkney Yole Association on 2 December 2000. A small North Isles yole (A & R Wilson) and several examples of South Isles yoles have since been built (I Richardson) and regularly compete on the regatta circuit.

Yoles and flatties hauled up at the Broad Noust and on Flaws' Pier, c.1968.

[In this next article, Maurice Davidson sheds light on why the Norse boats took different developmental routes in Orkney and Shetland, driven by the different sea conditions. He explains why Orkney went for a wide beamed, buoyant craft able to carry heavy loads. He also introduces us to the variants used down both the east and the west coast of Britain, which were all subject to similar Norse influences, showing how changes travelled both north and south to Orkney.]

LOCAL DEVELOPMENT OF YOLES IN AND AROUND ORKNEY by Maurice Davidson

Historical background

Small, narrow, shallow Norway yoles with sharp, curved stems and sterns were taken to Orkney by Vikings, probably from the mid 800s A.D., to be used for fishing and local isles transport. They came over with Viking refugees, fleeing from Norway, newly united (according to Saga) under a ruthless King Harald Finehair.[xxx]

The Norse ruled Orkney, Shetland, all the Western Isles (Sudreyjar) and Caithness, down to the Sutherland (Scotland) for many centuries, until Denmark pawned Orkney for 60,000 florins and Shetland for just 10,000 florins in 1468. Then, in 1470, came full annexation of the Northern Isles by Scotland, and Orkney's Scottification by the new Edinburgh lairds began.

Vikings formed trading partnerships wherever they invaded, all down the east coast of Scotland and England, with Peterhead, Deeside and Humberside all providing good harbour bases for winter. Stornoway, Belfast and Dublin were developed on the west coast.

Where the Norse went, so did their clinker longships and yoles. Boat repairing may easily lead to boat building by the local carpenters. So, we should not be surprised that clinker yoles or yawls – as the English, and even Caithness folk, call open, double ended, clinker boats – are still found on these coasts. Even the Norman - Northmen, Vikings from France - invasion of England in 1066 used longships, and Viking mercenaries towing a yole or two can be seen sewn into the Bayeux Tapestry.

Cheap imported yoles from Norway over time gave way to even cheaper, flat-packed strakes for construction in Orkney by the Earl or landowner's serf farmhands.

It was a small step then for the Earl or landowner to order his more skilled workers to copy the Norway yoles and build them locally, and more cheaply. From then on, the shape of the yole was slowly adapted to suit their uses and the local tidal conditions here. Timber was still imported from Norway, the Scottish mainland or, as time went on and trade developed, from the east Baltic states. Baltic countries needed fish, which Orkney had in plenty and could conveniently trade for timber, of which we have none.[xxxi]

Early development of yoles in Shetland and Orkney

Shetland, with its long sheltered voes and narrow sounds, needed little adaptation to the sleek Norway yole, or faering, to fit local conditions.

South Isles yole Gremsa and its older double Family Pride in the closely contested Longhope Regatta 2013. Gunter rigged Mohican in the lead.

It became a bit longer and wider, with more sheer topside, to lift to the sea swell, and more freeboard. The light, slim *Ness* and *Fair Isle yoals* still directly reflect their ancestors. Fair Isle was owned by Orkney (and Westray in particular) for centuries before Shetland gained ownership, and Westray skiffs may reflect the influence of the much sharper Fair Isle yoals.[xxxii]

Shetland yoles, and North Isles skiffs to a lesser extent, were rowing boats, designed to skim along the tide edges for fish. Shetland and the North Isles were poor and more isolated than Orkney, even in recent times past, and could not afford more efficient, modern sails or larger boats.

Orkney needed some further adaptations to these light Norway yoles, to cope with its stronger tides and to carry the larger and heavier farm loads here, across these turbulent sounds. Six to eight-knot tidal streams are found throughout Orkney in Hoy, Burra, Eynhallow, Burger Sounds, Papay Bore, Seal Skerry, Lashy, Calf, Warness, Copinsay, and Kirk Sounds (before the Barriers were built) with the Old Head, Liddle, Lother, Cantick, Brimsness, Torness, Swona, Stroma two miles south west (now part of Caithness) and the Pentland Skerries squeezing the Pentland Firth tides up to 12, and locally 16, knots. These give rise to massive tidal roosts[9] as the sea rushes round the Scottish mainland to fill the North Sea, then empty back out.

To cross our sounds, and connect our more scattered isles, a more buoyant yole is needed, with higher freeboard and more rounded, fuller bilges. To cross steep seas side-on, a wider yole is needed for yet more buoyancy and stability.

Rowing boats with slim V sections fore and aft would easily swamp, crossing side-on near the fast, rougher tidal roosts.

Two men could fish well from a 3.5 – 4.5 metre yole - or *quill*, as small, slim yoles with curved ends, more like wider Shetland yoles, were called locally. They were cheaper and used mainly for rowing, staying close to the shore and fishing cuithes and saithe for subsistence. They made a good crofters' boat for two, or four, folk in good weather, and were light enough to haul up their stony beach easily every night. These were the South Isles versions of the North Isles skiff.

More common was a 5.5-metre yole, double the volume of a quill, and a lot more seaworthy. This size of boat was normally shared between two neighbouring crofts or related families, as the cost of building and sailing such a boat was considerable. Four or six men could push out and heave a yole this size up a stony beach to the shelter of their noust[10], cut into the foreshore above high water. Their wives often helped with the hard labour onshore. And menfolk were often chided for having an easy time, sailing out west, with a brew and smoking all day. But they still had to be able to fish and sail well enough.

---

[9] Tidal overfalls with confused standing waves

[10] A place where a boat can be hauled up and kept ashore; specifically, a scooped-out shelter at the head of a stony shore well above high water, sometimes lined with a wall of stones

Wide, full Orkney yoles, for buoyancy, were used for piloting ships in the tidal Firth.
Daniell shows a two masted lugsail yole sailing off to catch the square-rigged ship.

The 5.5-metre yole could easily sail five miles offshore with the tide, and come ashore at night on the reverse tide, with a full boatload of four or six baskets of big cod, lythe, saithe and ling. All of these were good for splitting, salting, drying in the sun and keeping up in the roof timbers, to dry hard in the peat smoke. This provided high protein food for dark and windy winters. Without this store of fish, large families just could not exist in cold, hard times.

The first written records of Orkney show that some "fowereen" or four-oared yoles (faerings in Norway) and "sexaeringr" or six-oared yoles were still being imported in 1561 and 1566, despite Earl Stewart's ban on the import of "Norraway bots" in the mid-1500s to encourage local boatbuilding, and increase his profits [xxx]. By 1500, as the Scottish hand tightened, changes to Orkney's boats may already have been made, as only boats imported to Shetland were referred to as "Norraway bots".[xxxiii]

Shetland yoles are used to fish along the edges of their four- to six-knot tidal rips and nip over the generally narrow sounds, in comparative shelter behind their longer isles running north to south. Smaller sheep were the more common farm animals to be carried there, well suited to their slim yoles.

Orkney's wealthy Scottish lairds initially paid for the larger Orkney yoles, which were difficult to build as twisting the second and third strakes into larger curves is not easy. But this outlay ensured their cattle and farm produce arrived in good shape, and that the boats could land larger catches of cod and saithe for salting, to sell south.

By the 1570s, small Orkney yoles are recorded salting fish for Norway. Earl Stewart tried to control this trade and tax local boats for his coffers.[xxxiv]

By the 1600s, Norway regularly sent timber over to Orkney, which was traded for salt fish and farm produce. By this time many boats were built locally to a fuller Orkney design. In 1662 the Scot, Thomas Baikie of Kirkwall, is recorded as building a "great boat, thirty feet of keel with six huge strakes on each side of the hull, six fitted frames, with two standing lugsail masts and yards." This large boat was for the new Scottish laird on Stronsay to trade with Norway and join the cod fishing smacks offshore.

By the end of the 1700s, few Norwegian boats were imported to Orkney, cheap as they were, compared to Shetland which still bought 190 or so a year. Eventually, between 1807 and 1814, the Royal Navy blockaded Norway, as part of the Napoleonic War shipping restrictions. This ended the import of all Norway yoles and pine. Scots pine and larch were then used by local boatbuilders. [xxxi]

The use of sail drove the development of more powerful, wider and fuller yoles, slower to row even with four or six rowers. These wider boats provided a more stable base for sail. They also needed a deeper keel and steeper garboard strake above it, to make sure the boat did not just drift leeward, as the wind mainly pushes across the boat.

Daniell's 1820 print of square-sailed yoles and two lugsailed yoles in the Peerie Sea, Kirkwall, tending the sailing ships. The Peerie Sea later became Kirkwall's rubbish dump, now a pond.

Swaps, or stronger gusts of wind from the hills, can easily push you off course without this good, long, straight "grip o' the watter".

Sterns became deeper and angled, curved sternposts became straight, to take large rudders needed for easier manoeuvring under sail, but not necessary for rowing. Bows were fuller to avoid burying your yole into the sea in front as you ran before high seas, broaching and turning over as the wind howled.

Most folk here in Orkney sail only with the tide, for example going from Graemsay to Stromness with the ebb, then back with the flood (after selling a cow, buying seed and a nip or two in the Mason's Arms). So a sleek, fast yole is not needed, as the tide does most of the work for you. The wind in your sail does the rest of the work, no matter how heavy the boat or how many folk are onboard.

Development of yoles to the south and west of Orkney

The Appendix explores the development of yoles down the east coast of Scotland and England, and in the Western Isles and the North of Ireland. The developments were influenced primarily by local conditions and requirements. But some of these developments came back up north to Orkney, with the increase in fishing and money to develop boats down South influencing the design and build of yoles up here.

Differences between North and South Isles Orkney Yoles

Why, and how, the different parts of our Orkney isles have developed differing shapes of yoles is steeped in our seascape. North and South Isles were, and still are, isolated from each other by the Mainland of Orkney, with no easy yole sea route round the Mainland.

So, influences from Shetland, in the north, and Scotland to the south were easily isolated by the poverty of crofting everywhere.

Most yoles were built by crofters for cheapness, but some isles such as Stroma, Flotta, Westray and Sanday had recognised, skilled boatbuilders who built boats full time. This is where yole design developed, by use and practice.

Smaller four- to five-metre **Westray skiffs** are really rowing boats, sitting low on the water, with a narrow 1.3 metre beam for double oar rowing, more vertical stems to keep the bows sharp, and very raked, straight rudder posts for a longer boat. All this gives little buoyancy but provides length and easy speed, as can be seen on regatta day.

Sail has deepened these skiffs' sterns, as it has in our yoles, to avoid leeway in a wind. Skiffs have a very similar shape to huge Zulu fishing boats and to the smaller original, clinker Zulu skiff tenders of the late 1800s, which were a regular visitor to Pierowall's sheltered bay in Westray. They were well suited for a couple of crofters to row out north to fish, then sail back with a simple dipping lugsail, heavy with haddock. The isles were poor because of isolation; hence a smaller, light skiff was all they could afford.

Perhaps they were also influenced by dozens of Fair Islers, with their lean yoles, who emigrated to Westray in the famines of the 1800s. Fair Isle was part of the Brough lairdship in Westray for many years.

North isles yole Lizzie 2 in close competition with the South isles yole Helga at the Kirkwall Regatta in 2008. In lighter winds the more slender North Isles yoles and skiffs are faster.

North isles yole Lizzie 2, a new replica of their old family yole with vertical bow, very raked stern and narrow, shallow hull. Sailed (and built) by Andrew and Richard Wilson c.2010.

North Isles yoles are similar in size to their cousins in the South Isles, but with a narrower beam of 1.8 or 2 metres. They are designed for the same jobs, carrying a variety of heavy goods from farm and fish, across fast, tidal sounds.

Like the skiffs, they have more vertical stems, which makes for a smooth bow with less flare, and a boat that is easier to build, but wet. 'Timmers', as frames are called locally, are usually fitted, alternating two-thirds of the way across the floor or two-thirds of the way down from the gunwales. This resulted in a cheap, flexible, Norway yole build.

Their single standing lugsails are simple and cheap to use, again as seen on fishing boats from Shetland and the South.

Sanday yoles sometimes have slightly curved sternposts and a narrower beam, also like Shetland yoles.

South Isles yoles have more sheer and flare, to keep them dry, than their Northern cousins. They have a far more curved bow for lighter ends, more buoyancy, and to beach easily with dry feet. Stern posts are straight and steeply raked for a large rudder – following Moray scaffies, which fished round these shores. Sterns are deeper and fuller than in the North Isles, again to maximise buoyancy, as you sail back with a load of fish through the tides.

Fishermen are usually keen to learn from others, and observe what works. Their lives depend on it!

Ample rounded bilges, with vertical sides and a 2.2 metre beam, give good buoyancy for sailing across the more tidal seas here as you near the Pentland Firth, the tides speeding up round the big Scottish mainland.

Early yoles had garboards at 45 degrees to their keel, midships, to gain beam without draught, like ships' boats. Later as sail developed, and distances offshore got longer to find fish or ships to pilot, garboards became more vertical. This kept a straighter course and gave less leeway in blustery winds. And the winds are always blustery in Orkney.

Fitted oak timmers were usual on yoles, full width across the keel, alternating to the garboard, every 250mm or so. This provides strength for this more rounded hull, as it lifts over the waves. Steamed oak timmers became more usual after World War II.

Yoles became larger as catches increased, and fish merchants from Scotland came here to buy both fresh and salted, dried cod for Spain and the Baltic. As inshore seas were cleared, yoles had to sail further offshore and lay miles of heavy gret lines[11] in deeper water, again needing larger yoles. They also fished more using heavier flag and iron creels, for lobsters.

---

[11] Long lines of baited hooks

OYA South Isles yole Lily with traditional three spreet (sprit) sail rig and flattie tender on a mooring in Stromness harbour. 2019 regatta.

South Isles yoles used two unstayed masts and two sprit sails, or 'spreet' sails as they are called locally, for quick furling, giving clear areas for fishing plus faster tacking round all the isles, not just sailing in and out to sea. Bowsprits and jibs might be used in light summer winds, for extra speed.

Ten to eleven larch strakes were common to most yoles, with skiffs using nine to ten and larger yoles maybe thirteen strakes, when heavy engines were used, though this number was superstitiously avoided by many.

Stromness had the most ships' pilots in the whole of Scotland to navigate large ships safely through the Pentland Firth and Scapa Flow, avoiding rocks and tidal roosts. In the mid-1800s there were 23 pilots, typically using six rowers in a larger six-metre, fast yole with spritsails, kept in the Broad Noust below what is now the Orkney Yole Association sail house. Baikie's boatyard next door specialised in building over 160 large and fast yoles until World War I.

Swona and Stroma yoles became larger, and much fuller along all the length of their hull, giving very rounded bows and sterns. They were more like a buoyant ship's lifeboat, which would be seen on passing square riggers, piloted by these islanders through the turbulent Pentland Firth, but with a deeper, more vertical garboard and keel for sail. They were built to survive long sails out and back from these ships, sometimes with lumpy seas in the strong tide here, with nowhere to hide.[xxxv]

Again, fishermen were quick to copy things that worked, from ships they worked on.

Yoles may have come in from Norway, but the development of Orkney yoles seems to have been more influenced by fishing boats from Moray, Aberdeen, and Yorkshire.

All Orkney yoles remain light, sharp ended, buoyant and flexible, thanks to their thin clinker build. They have the merit of being cheap to build in a small outhouse by handy crofters. This buoyancy enables them to earn their keep, whether carrying fish, farm food or animals, peat, coal or folk across the many fast tides to the town.

THE HARBOUR STROMA

The Haven or Hofn pier and shingle noust on Stroma, showing their many very rounded, three sailed, spreet (sprit) yoles hauled up by hand above the high water. Fishing was major here. c.1898.

[The Orkney yole today is usually powered by sail, with a back-up outboard or inboard engine – and hardly ever rowed. The editor's own attempts at rowing have been hampered by (a) a gunter rig getting in the way (b) the wide beam making it very difficult for one rower to man two oars and (c) the sheer weight of the vessel. But Maurice Davidson's article below shows how they were originally designed for oars, and then sails added in different configurations as generations found the rigs best suited to the then use. Maurice explains the shift to engine after World War I – and then the return to more traditional sail as use changed from work to leisure.]

YOLE OARS, SAILS AND ENGINE by Maurice Davidson

From the beginning, oars were used to move yoles. The size of yoles and the number of thwarts or seats was adapted according to the number of rowers. Shetland yoles had single banked rowers with one or two oars, as they were only 1 to 1.3 metres wide, and were rowed single- or, in the case of 'fowereens', double-handed with four oars. Wider 'sixareens' had six single-handed oars and a helmsman.[xxxvi]

Orkney yoles could only be rowed double banked as they were much wider, being 2 metres or up to even 3 metres wide in Swona/Stroma yoles, so designed for four or six crew, and perhaps an old hand at the tiller.

Traditional Viking square sails were still used in Shetland up until the late 1800s, but then changed to the offset version of dipping lugsails, so as to go better to windward. These lugsails were introduced by southern fishing boats coming up into Shetland's abundant grounds.

Then, to sail even faster in light winds, jibs were set out forward on long bowsprits and unstayed masts pulled further to the bow. Lugsails were tucked down to the masts, instead of the bow, and the standing lugsail invented. Southern boats again led the way, and Orkney followed, as they were easier to tack into the wind and simple and cheap to use. Isles folk have never been slow to learn if they see an advantage which can be adapted to the harsher weather there.

Smaller North Isles skiffs, and their larger yoles, mainly use a single, unstayed mast, with **standing lugsail** and a flying jib, recently changing to sloop sails for regattas. South Isles also used standing lugsails in smaller quills, but developed **sprit sails or spreet sails** as they are called locally, probably after seeing them in visiting navy ships' boats in the course of the late 1700s wars – these being used to chase fishermen and forcibly press gang them into the Navy.

Sprit sails are much easier to tack when sailing around Orkney's many isles. They head you closer into the wind than lugsails and are quicker to wrap round the mast out of the way to fish.

The bowsprit jib is hung from the top of the taller foremast, with a loose-footed foresail supported by the diagonal sprit to the rear. A tarry rope, the **shangie,** loops round the mast to hold the spreet end. The mainsail normally is smaller and tied on a small boom to flatten the sail when going to windward. Interestingly, Trondheim, and many other Scandinavian yoles, also use spritsails for easy tacking.

South Isles spreet (sprit) sailed yoles Frances and Gremsa rowing into the Corpach locks at the Caledonian Canal during the Great Glen Raid 2001.

Seen from behind, they form a more flexible split square sail set on two masts.[xxxvii] Two standing masts give easier-sized sails to handle out at sea and a wide area between the masts for fishing and gear.

Post war single gunter or sloop rigged masts on yoles allow you to sail a lot closer to the wind and are a huge advantage in regatta courses, but not at sea. The more central mast with long boom and gunter gets in the way of fish and the crew. The much taller mast needs wire stays for support, and makes the yole roll a lot more at sea, especially at moorings, to damp which ballast has to be placed in the hull.

Traditionally, solid pine masts sit in a shoe on the keel, and are supported by a heavy thwart, with round slot and locking pin. Thafts, as seats or thwarts are called locally, are clinched to a good hand-sized wiring, or stringer, to spread the mast loads, and to haul up the beach. This is another reason why yoles are shallow and without side decks, as arms are only so long!

Every night masts would be laid down on the thwarts, so they were sized to the yole length. Barked brown canvas sails would be hung to dry in the sail house at the noust[12]. Yoles were only set on moorings and rowed out to in quiet summer weeks, until later, when engines appeared and this became a more regular occurrence.

Between World War I and World War II all yoles changed to using petrol or paraffin engines, for sheer convenience. Sails were laid up in sail houses and forgotten. However, a pair of oars and a small lugsail were kept onboard, just in case of engine problems. These yoles were now usually moored in summer, as they were too heavy to haul up beaches, even on linns[13]. An extra strake was usually added to raise the gunwales, now that yoles sat deeper in the sea.

Ironically, at the present time there is only one Orkney yole still fishing with an engine, but ten or more sailing yoles. This is a huge change from between the wars, when over 300 yoles, mainly with engines, were in regular use here. [xxx]

Yoles in Norway are still oiled in boiled spruce sap, which soaks into the wood to prevent water and rot entering. Inevitably this goes dark brown, or takes on a reddish hue when fishermen used cod liver oil from fish they caught. Hence the popular house colours in the north of Norway. Oil was used here until good quality lead paint became freely available – from the Northern Lighthouse Board.

Lots of left over half-used drums of white, red, green and black paint used on all navigation buoys and lighthouses round Orkney could be had, and even more became available once the lead-painted *Pole Star* lighthouse vessel was based in Stromness.

So dark oils were replaced by white strakes, with red or green rubbing strakes for decoration. Paint, however, only covers the surface and does not preserve the wood. Black coal tar sealed the insides, with red Northern Lighthouse Board anti-foul below the waterline for moored yoles. Isles cottages were all painted similar Northern Lighthouse Board colours and looked very smart.

---

[12] A boat haul, a shallow depression where Orkney yoles were overwintered

[13] Wooden tracks

2013 Deerness Boat Show with the Papay lugsail yole Fly, 15' long, belonging to Peter Miller, Kirkwall.

[The original version of this article by Arthur Johnston appeared in Yachting World in July 1936 and was reproduced in The Orcadian in October of that year. It gives an interesting perspective from shortly before the Second World War. We have edited the wording slightly to make it easier on the eye of today's reader, but have not changed the content. The Ness yole referred to below is a Shetland boat. As Maurice Davidson has explained in an earlier article, the Shetland conditions led to their boats being designed primarily as fast rowing boats for fishing, similar to our North Isles skiffs. The Orkney yawl described below is our Orkney yole.]

THE NESS YOLE AND THE ORKNEY YAWL – two northern types of boat by Arthur Johnston

These boats from the Northern Isles each have a clear Viking origin. Their diverging evolution in hull-shape and rig reflects the developing uses to which they have been put. The Ness yawl is perhaps the closer to the original type of longboat used by the early Norwegian settlers. Although it is smaller, it is still used for very similar sea work – rowing as easily as possible in the sort of wild water that results from hard wind against strong tides.

The Orkney boat, however, needed a greater capacity for carrying. This entailed a stiffer section and a broader beam suitable for sailing; rowing was a secondary function. Fishing was usually carried out near the coast or in the narrows, where the current is strong and the sea in a gale deeper, heavier and more broken. Even over the banks much further out, the shallowness of the water causes a heavier sea – a dangerous situation for the fisherman.

Ness Yole - Rowing only

The Ness Yole, or Jol, hails from Dunrossness, in the most southerly part of Shetland, which gives it its name. A long, low, narrow boat mostly used for fishing, it is unique to this district.

Saithe, also known as coal fish, were commonly caught by this boat. Two men would row, each with an oar. Two others, one forward and one in the stern, fished with a line thrown out on the tide side. The oarsmen row, or 'andoo' as they call it, as steadily as they can while the other two watch the lines. When the tide is running hard, these float near the surface of the water.

As the tide becomes weaker, the fish go deeper, and a sinker, weighing about 1½ pounds, is used to let the hooks go down to about 20 fathoms (36 metres). They are then hauled up as quickly as possible, to simulate the movement of escaping prey, and they are easily taken. The fishermen call this method dragging for fish.

Rigged with a square sail and a mast near the centre, these boats might be described as the true 'Norway Yawls', having very much the build and character of whale boats. They were handled in a wonderful manner by the Shetlanders, who, in their love for the sea and by their daring and energy on it, show themselves still worthy of that descent from the Norsemen of which they are all so proud.

2012 photo of Stroma yole stern showing the wide curving clinker lines to give good buoyancy.
Now used for creel fishing out of Wick.

Fast tides

Round Sumburgh Head and the many points and promontories between the rocks and islands, the dangerous tideway known as the roost runs at a terrific rate, and in these boats they will 'cut the string', which means crossing these tideways.

Usually this is only attempted at slack tides, but when necessity arises, and it has to be done at full tides, the danger is extreme.

Sometimes they crushed the livers of the fish to make oil and prevent the sea breaking and often had to 'up and off' owing to the suddenness of a storm and either row for hours to make the land or scud before it under bare poles.

Inferior Orcadian boats 150 years ago

Around 150 years ago, the boat in use throughout Orkney was much inferior in model, construction and rig to those of the present day. The smaller boats in use then were low, flattish things with straight stem and sternpost raking considerably, and fastened with tree nails. They carried one sail, sometimes two, very often with oars doing the work.

Orcadians are not all perhaps such thoroughbred fishermen as the Shetlanders and were somewhat reluctant to follow this hazardous profession, farming being their main industry.

Orkney Yole uses - General Transport

The Orkney boats were often used for general purposes, such as carrying fuel across the sounds, taking corn to the mill, shipping kelp or transporting provisions. In the older boats there was little enthusiasm for fishing, given the rapid tides among the isles and the frequent bad weather – serious handicaps to men not used to boats and gear.

The later Orkney boat carries a jib and two large lugsails. Usually, the after lug is rigged with a boom. Although they are the same type as the old 'straight stems', they are remarkably improved. The stem has now a fine curve, the hold is deeper and the mould fuller. They are now copper fastened throughout, and painted or varnished instead of being tarred.

Orcadians also used to rig them with spritsails, which they apparently found to be both handy and safe. These were often used in boats with an 11ft to 15ft keel, for general use and for lobster and line fishing. The sail was laced to the mast, and they were taken ashore together after each trip out.

Piloting is another Orcadian venture. Today it is carried out with motor boats, but before this larger 15ft to 18ft vessels sailed far out from land in the hope of picking up ships and navigating them past the dangerous island waters. They used to have 30 to 36 foot herring fishing boats, but they have long since been abandoned, and hardly any Orkney boats fish for herring today.

With a population scattered over a number of islands, boats are an essential way of connecting them, so they will always have a role to play, navigating tides which in some places run to six or seven knots. It used to be said, and may still be said of Orcadians, that they can hardly step over their threshold without their boats.

2016, yoles hand-loaded onto the North Isles ferry all for the Westray Regatta. The Shetland boat high on the rear trailer is a slim and fast rowing yoal, compared to the Orkney yoles.

[In this next article, Maurice builds on the developments in yole design (which he has previously described) to tell us about specific adaptations in Stroma and Swona, two islands in the middle of the Pentland Firth, whose turbulent waters made it imperative to have particularly seaworthy vessels. It is interesting to note how design elements from East coast boats were incorporated. Sadly, both isles, along with other isles in the south of Orkney, are now abandoned and their yole heritage is history.]

STROMA AND SWONA YOLES by Maurice Davidson

Over 250 years ago, Duncan's boat yard started building large wooden yoles in Burray, for the booming cod fishery on the East side, and for the Pentland Firth. Forced here by the French war down south, English smacks were coming up for cod and buying fish from local yoles, salting fish on the beaches. Duncan's took in all the techniques from larger East Coast fishing boats, and adapted them to our smaller yoles. A larger, more buoyant, rounded and heavily bilged hull was developed, able to carry larger catches of fish. This was essentially a ship's lifeboat with curved bow and angled stern, to save wood, lighten ends to lift over the seas, and keep costs down. [xxxv]

A couple of Stroma boatbuilders at Duncan's, Smith and Banks, went back to Stroma and built these yoles on the isle. They started with the standard four to six man, 5.5 metres long by 2.2 metres wide yoles, with 4 metres of keel. But as cod fishing in the Pentland Firth was good, and winches started to appear on the shores from wrecked ships, the laird ordered a larger yole for fishing and his transport.

After the Napoleonic wars, in the 1840s or so, fish merchants appeared here too and offered fishermen a better deal. They could have a loan for their own yole and gear, as long as they sold all the fish to the fish merchant. The remains of Robertson's fish merchant store are still at the head of their common noust in Stroma.

Independence from the laird brought huge increases in fish output as people could see they would gain not just for the laird but for themselves. Larger and more powerful yoles were built by the many boat builders on Stroma, adapted to long distance piloting and creeling around the Skerries, some up to 7.5 metres long, 3 metres wide with 12 to 13 strakes.[xxxviii]

These yoles were similar to, but stronger than, the large, wide, open Moray Firth scaffies nearby, which maximised the carrying capacity for a given length. And of course, yoles were light enough and buoyant enough to go over steep, lumpy swells side on, as is necessary round a tidal island. The length of boat was the maximum a small isle community could winch or haul up a beach each night, as there was no pier or harbour in Stroma, before the lighthouse was built.

Most Stroma yole photographs show that lugsails gave way to more controllable ***spreetsails*** (spritsails), then engines. Foredecks strengthened the bows for their long foremasts and large spreetsails, which led to fully decked yoles with hatches for work areas, all following the larger, decked fishing boats from the south. The Moray scaffies' timber head frames above the deck were adopted to strengthen the gunwales, all as seen on today's remaining yoles.

Large 20 foot Stroma yole Kelvin Star, still used for lobster creeling out of Keiss, Caithness, seen here at Wick marina, 2012. The very wide beam can be seen with a curved sheer.

All the Stroma yoles were flat, with little sheer, again like ship's boats, which reduced wind drift when fishing, and cut costs. Stroma crofters may have had more money than most, but they were still poor, and under the debt monopoly of their Scottish laird.

Life on much smaller Swona, a couple of miles to the North East across the narrowing Firth, was lonelier, but similar to Stroma. Here the Rosie family also built similar large, buoyant, round-shouldered yoles on the isle, some up to 7.5 metres long.

It must be emphasized that no one ever sails into a roost - tidal overfalls, confused standing waves - however mild or wild. Their shape, size and whereabouts are all known and looked out for, so that they can be avoided.

Swona and Stroma yoles were designed for their uses, not just for strong tides nearby, as they often smooth the sea. They were mainly used for the huge catches of fish they could make next to these strong tide eddies, or for sailing a long 10 or 15 miles to catch a ship and pilot for good money and sail back – but not always on the same day, or week! They were also used for ferrying a load of passengers 20 miles across the Firth and back, with no shelter if the wind picks up.

They were even used to salvage a few bits of brass and the odd cargo from a nearby wreck! They made some extra money from this, yes, but they had to take many risks. Big, strong yoles reduced this risk. There were no wealthy fishermen in yoles! [xxxv]

They could afford larger, locally made yoles and needed such boats to make sure they all survived. With their extra money, the Stroma men adapted their yoles to elliptical sterns, longer and faster like the famous Lipton yachts. These were more manoeuvrable when fitted with an inboard rudder, but this was not welcomed by everyone, as lacking buoyancy aft. And how do you clear a creel rope round the hidden rudder or prop?

Stroma pirates were well known, as they were always the first to get to a wrecked ship in the Firth, and there were many in this crowded and turbulent seaway. The lure of making a quick pound to pay off the debt on their large boat or home, was too much for poor crofting folk. Stroma and Swona folk were not alone in this stripping of wrecks. Everyone was at it, from the laird and minister taking their cargo share as landlord and minder, merchants drinking cheap, salt-laced port and wine, or crofters using deck timber, washed up on the shore, to extend their *peedie hoose* (small house).

It was little wonder that, in the late 1880s recession, with low prices for fish, many of Stroma's 341 inhabitants quickly emigrated to escape their poverty. More left after the economic depression that followed World War I. Finally, the isle was abandoned, despite the council building a small enclosed harbour in the 1950s. This served the laird and his sheep, but not the rest of the folk. There was nothing on the other side to make yole landings easier and rents were still rising as they had a pier now! Good, regular wages could instead be had in Dounreay Nuclear Reactor at this point.[xxxix]

This story was repeated time and again in Orkney's smaller isles, as young folk refused to accept the hardship of a crofter's life, where you never own and control your livelihood.

Willie Mowatt in 2010 beside his grandfather's 134 year old Stroma yole.
The Star of Burwick is light and low for fishing or easy hauling ashore.

Only the scale of Stroma makes it different. With old age and illness, the three Rosies of Swona finally abandoned their isle in 1974, leaving animals, good houses and their big 7.5 metre elliptic sterned yole *Hood*, stranded above the only Hofn, or Haven, landing geo[14].

Faray, Cava, Fara and Copinsay all followed in silence now, all abandoned after World War II, as young folk sought better opportunities elsewhere. Wild and lonely Pentland Skerries, and Sule Skerry 36 miles out West, were also abandoned by lightkeepers and donkeys, as cost-cutting automation proceeded in the 1990s.

Funded by the Northern Lighthouse Board to transport lighthouse keepers and cargo, a large 8.5 metre sprit-sailed yole, built in Orkney in c.1865, serviced the Skerries. This could be the largest Orkney yole ever built. She was winched up the shingle beach at Burwick noust, and ended her days in the loch there, flipped up and over the road in a hurricane. It is ironic that the largest yole was built for the smallest inhabited isle in Orkney!

---

[14] A rocky inlet, which can provide suitable shelter

2012 photo of Willie Bremner's old Stroma-type yole lying at the YM Hall, Longhope, now being restored on Flotta.

Freddie Young, Stromness with one of Alex Young's original Orkney flatties c.1890.
Design said to be taken from the Newfoundland Banks stacking cod fish boats.

[In this next article, Maurice makes a detour from yoles to introduce the two types of tenders with which they are most often associated.]

PRAAMS AND FLATTIES by Maurice Davidson

PRAAMS

Praams are very curved, clinker-built tenders, with two cut-off ends and little or no keel; so they can be hauled up shallow shores. They were often carried on Norse fishing boats, visiting Orkney. These are descendants of original flat-bottomed carvel river boats, with no keel at all, which are still used in Eastern Europe. [xxxviii]

The smaller, 3-metre-long tenders were developed after World War I by North Ronaldsay fishermen, who had no good mooring shores for motor boats, hence had to haul their yoles up the steep shores every night. Inshore, creel fishing praams were 4 to 5 metres in length with 1.5 to 1.8 metre beam, flat bows and transoms, handy for hitching light outboard engines on. They had plenty of buoyancy, ideal for motoring heavy creels round the rocks. With double bilge keels and a small keel, they could get into shallow water and easily be hauled up the steep, stony beaches above the highwater line with a Ferguson tractor.

At sea, the praams were very manoeuvrable and buoyant, with wide, curved bottoms and curved ends to ride over inshore seas. But this very lack of direction-keeping, and rolly, rounded stability, limited them to a few enthusiasts on North Ronaldsay. Yet again, praams show how observant fishermen are, ready to change if they see an advantage. The extent of the ache in your shoulders, when hauling boats ashore, and your very life may depend on this.

FLATTIES

Stromness developed quite narrow and long, flat-bottomed boats, as tenders to larger moored yoles in this sheltered harbour, being spared North Ronaldsay's problems. Tradition says that flatties were based on Newfoundland's cod fishing dories, seen stacked on deck, on the large bluenose schooners, some 150 years ago or so.

Small square sails were sometimes used on these flatties, which were 3 to 5 metres long and 1 to 1.3 metres wide. With a draught of 10 centimetres and a slightly curved, flat bottom, flatties get you onto the shore with dry feet. The curved bottom avoids catching on all the stones and slipways, when launching and hauling up.

Many British estuaries and rivers also developed flatties, in a very similar way, as tenders and ferries to ensure dry feet. They even have clinker sides. Thus, flatties may have also come up on southern fisher boats, rather than from the romantic West.[xl]

Many young folk spent all summer in these small, light flatties as a great introduction to the sea, rowing and fishing for sillocks. Heavier engined yoles were moored off the isles' shores in the summer, and flatties became a cheap and popular tender everywhere. They were also handy for setting illegal trout nets in the shallows, to earn a quiet shilling or two from tourist hotels - providing some pocket money. One of these early flatties decorates the ceiling of the Flattie Bar in the Stromness Hotel! Why is there no Yole Bar?

North Ronaldsay praam built 1920, used for lobster fishing at Dennis Head beacon, North Ronaldsay, c.2000. Transom stern handy for hanging light outboard engine, and hauling up beach.

[In this next article, Ron Bulmer builds on the Norse connections of the Orkney yole by introducing us to the activities of Norway's Coastal Foundation and finding similarities between our Orkney yole and the Norwegian snekke and other traditional boats still being built in Sweden. We are hopeful that Orkney as well as Shetland can link into their UNESCO proposal to maintain the common heritage of wooden clinker-built boats.]

UNESCO INTANGIBLE CULTURAL HERITAGE, THE KYSTEN FORBUNDET AND THE ORKNEY YOLE ASSOCIATION
by Ron Bulmer

For people living next to the sea, communities have a special connection, particularly when history gives a direct lineage. The British Isles and Norway in particular share this in outlook, etymology, and heritage … and to visit the Northern Isles of Orkney and Shetland, is to find there still remains a sense of injustice that the islands were never returned to the Norwegian Crown. Indeed, when speaking to an elderly neighbour after the 2014 referendum for Scotland's independence, I quizzed her about wanting to remain in the Union. And then, unable to stop myself, I asked: "Suppose the referendum were to re-join Norway?"

"Oh", she replied, "That would have been quite different".

And so it is, that in the Orkney dialect there remain many words with Scandinavian roots – but the most tangible evidence of connection is the traditional clinker-built boats.

Norway still has a very strong tradition of building boats in wood. As such, boatbuilders are found the length and breadth of the Norwegian coastline – with the help and support of the Kysten Forbundet, probably best translated as the Coastal Foundation.

Kysten Forbundet supports not just traditional boat building, but other coastal traditions too.

A submission has recently been made to UNESCO, in support of intangible cultural heritage [ICH] through traditional clinker-built boats, which is a great testament to a collaborative effort right across Scandinavia. What is even more noteworthy, is that this is the first collaborative application to UNESCO. The Ministries of Culture of Norway, Sweden, Denmark, Finland, Iceland, including the Faroes and Åland Islands, have all supported the submission – as part of the North Sea Ring – an exemplary example of promoting a common culture and heritage.

Encouragingly, the UK Parliament is now considering ratifying the UNESCO Convention on the Protection of the Intangible Cultural Heritage. On 17 March 2021, there was a meeting with representatives from various interest groups, where this was discussed.

Eivind Falk, Director from the Norwegian Crafts Institute, was asked what Norway has gained from ratifying the convention. In reply, Eivind emphasized how the convention contributes to focusing on continuation and protection, and could lead to an increased status for traditional crafts in Norway. In his post, Eivind also emphasized how the NGOs' role had been strengthened, and how the convention has helped to lift the entire field nationally and internationally. He says:

"So far, 180 of UNESCO's 193 member states have ratified the Convention on the Protection of the Intangible Cultural Heritage from 2003. It would have been great if we could now contribute to the UK ratification. Based on the rich craft traditions and the commitment, it would be nice to welcome them into the family."[15]

Norway's approach to supporting this intrinsic heritage is through the Kysten Forbundet. Kysten Forbundet's motto 'Preservation through Use', certainly rings true with the Orkney Yole Association. However, they have a much wider brief than boats, and actively safeguard the traditional crafts industries and infrastructure along Norway's lengthy coastline.

Forbundet Kysten has an enviable record, engaging staff, academic research and support, but importantly has a solid community base, especially museums and schools, ensuring a continuity of heritage.

Orkney, being an archipelago, has developed similar strong avenues of heritage preservation – though I think it is fair to say that it does not have an overarching federation in the way Kysten Forbundet has.

The Viking Longboat is a familiar image to most: the long, sleek, highly seaworthy, yet versatile vessel, with the flex to manage substantial sea crossings, yet shallow enough draught to row up river estuaries, or, if necessary, be dragged overland.

However, the Scandinavians were (and still are!) an adaptable people. While the *langskip* [longship] is the iconic vessel, there was also the cargo vessel or variously *kogg* or *knarr*[16], which was designed to carry considerable cargo, and required perhaps as little as one-metre draught, enabling approach and landing in shallow coastal waters. And the shape of the Orkney yole is becoming evident.

Notice that *langskip*, *knarr* and yole are all clinker built. Further, like so many traditional crafts, the skills were passed from one generation to the next, as an oral tradition. And in Orkney, there is now only one proficient professional boat builder in wood, when, not so many years ago, most communities would have had several, with boats being built as winter projects in sheds.

The Orkney Historic Boat Society raised a bursary to ensure that Orkney retained the boat building tradition, as well as preserving a remarkable maritime history, that was all too close to being lost altogether. The Orkney Yole Association encourages the sailing of the yole, ideally with a three sailed traditional rig – the more contemporary gunter rig is looked on askance by the dyed-in-the-wool traditionalists! Both organisations are fine examples of preservation and conservation, served by dedicated volunteers.

In corresponding with Kysten Forbundet, a style of boat, the *snekke*, which is common in the south of the country, was highlighted. *Snekke* also means 'carpenter'. Although now exclusively motor

---

[15] Norsk håndverksinstituttet.

[16] https://www.danishnet.com/vikings/types-viking-ships/

driven, the *snekke* has close lines to the yole. Further, the motor *snekke* is predominantly found in the municipality of Stavern.

It is interesting to compare the lines of a south isles yole, and a motor *snekke*. The drawing below is of *Family Pride,* an Orkney yole:

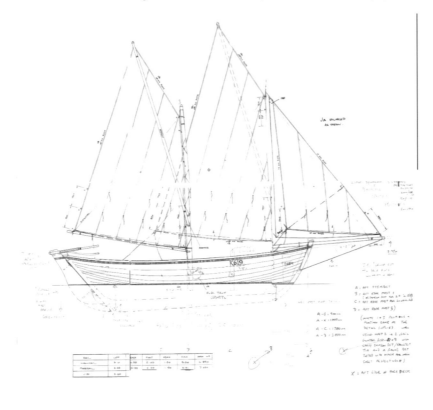

The drawing is reproduced courtesy of Dennis Davidson.

Snekker were once workboats, but today are pleasure boats that can be found across Norway as well as on the west coast of Sweden and in the Baltic. The type is native to Oslofjord and the Skagerrak, ranging from Mandal, the southernmost city in Norway, to Fredrikstad near the Swedish border. The modern snekke developed from the slightly smaller oar-and-sail-driven traditional workboats of the same name. With the addition of engines in the 1910s, the tiller-steered open double-enders became "motorsnekke," which are a little longer and fuller—particularly in the stern—than their forebears, and have higher freeboard to accommodate the extra power and weight. Still, they bear a close resemblance to them.[17]

The drawings on the page opposite are of a motorsnekke, courtesy of 'Wooden Boat' magazine.

Indeed, there are differences to a yole – which in all probability will cause much heated debate – but the similarity has to be noted. And it was only thanks to the keen recreational sailor that Orkney yoles were again sailed and engines [usually outboards] were kept for back-up.

Travelling into west Sweden, a coastline noted for archipelagoes – the cargo vessel again has a familiarity – see drawing opposite.

---

[17] Eelyvn Ansel *The Snekke Norway's timeless motor launch* WoodenBoat. Note 'snekker' is the plural of 'snekke'.

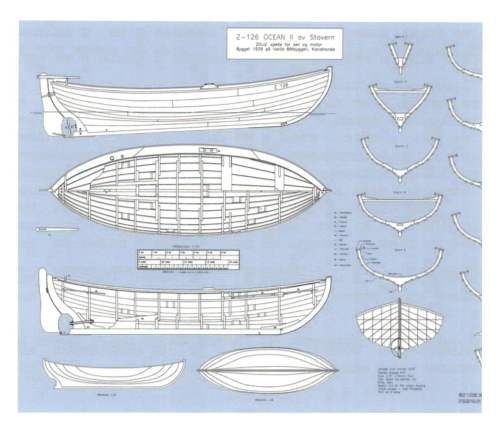

skrev Kystlaget Fredriksvern

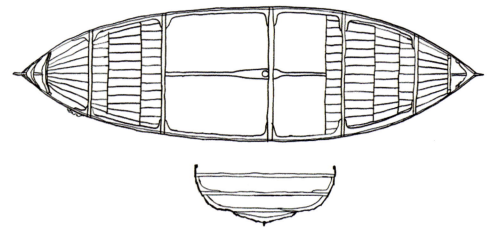

https://regia.org/research/ships/Ships0.htm

And to quote from a Classic Boat article: 'Sweden's oldest fishing boat restored': "[These were] clearly Viking merchant ships. The largest was 16.5 meters long, built of pine and it could carry up to 40 tonnes of goods. Traces of similar merchant ships have been found in Åskeskårr in Western Sweden, near Kaupang in Norway, and in the harbour of Hedeby. All these ships have similar characteristics. They were all *broader in proportion* to their length than the warships. They had a wider and deeper hull for cargo, and they were clearly *much more dependent on the sail than the oars*. Speed for these vessels was clearly not a priority. The real *priority was to have a seaworthy vessel* which could cross vast stretches of ocean without wreck. The oars would probably only have been used to help the ship in and out of harbour. These ships *probably operated along the coasts of Scandinavia and in the open seas to the west"*. [Italics are mine]

They were probably somewhat bigger than the trustworthy Orkney yole, but such links should not be too far-fetched. It also shows the real possibility of the commonality of similar boats along the east coast of the British Isles.

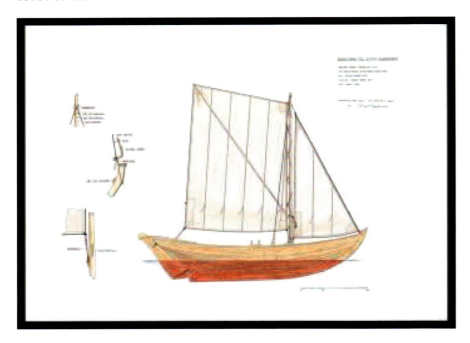

Source: Båtritningar Handelsbolag Björkenäs Jämjö Sweden

On Sweden's southern coast line, drawings [see above and across], show examples of vessels of that familiar shape. Note the sprit sail, though almost square here, and double head sail, but these are not unknown in Orkney waters. This family business offers not just the line drawings, but a complete boat.

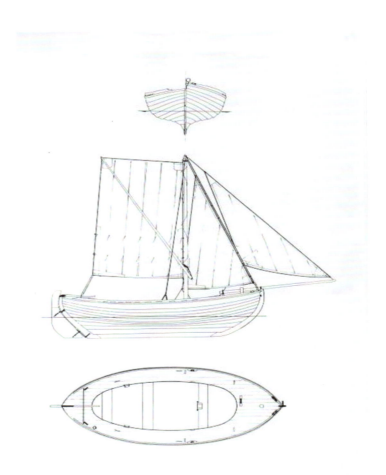

Source: Båtritningar Handelsbolag Björkenäs Jämjö Sweden

This small treatise is not intended to draw a conclusion, but to raise a further sense of enquiry as to the derivation of the noble clinker-built yole. Evidence points towards a commonality of design with boats still afloat along southern Scandinavian coastlines. Is there sufficient weight of evidence to draw a positive conclusion? Not without delving further - and indeed, as with many vernacular traditions, a gut feeling is probably our best [and only] guide.

Acknowledgements and References:

Tove Aurdal Hjellnes, Forbundet Kysten
Jeff Mackie, Stromness Boat Builder
Ian Richardson, retired Stromness boatbuilder
James Clouston, Chair: Orkney Historic Boat Society
Lars A Solberg, Kystlaget Fredriksvern Norway
Roger Andersson, Båtritningar Handelsbolag Björkenäs Jämjö Sweden
Classic Boat July 2017: 'Sweden's oldest fishing boat restored' by Susanne Ravanis, with photos c/o the Ravanis family and Lars Jansson
Eelyvn Ansel The *Snekke Norway's timeless motor launch* WoodenBoat
Nordic Clinker Boat UNESCO Nomination
Request by a Non-Governmental Organisation to be Accredited to provide Advisory Services to the Committee UNESCO ICH-09-Form deadline 31 May 2015
https://www.danishnet.com/vikings/types-viking-ships/
https://regia.org/research/ships/Ships0.htm

Stromness Primary School P6 and P7 young folk out for their first sail. They all helm, pull the ropes and make our day full of smiles all round.

[This next article by Ron Bulmer explores the Orkney yole's Scandinavian links through linguistic similarities in its name.]

YOLE, YOAL OR YAWL? GIVE THE YAWL A SMAKK By Ron Bulmer

Photos provided by Boat Building Academy Lyme Regis

The Orcadian dialect has a wonderful expression [it is a very rich dialect] – 'that's a raffle'. In other words, 'that's something of a muddle '– and the word 'yole' is no exception. This raffle is compounded by the vagaries of the English language, and its adopted patterns of usage. By contrast, the French have the rightly famous Académie Française[18], ensuring rigour with the French language, but they are not alone. Norway has Det Norske Akademi[19], which regulates Riksmål[20], the official language, and is responsible for publishing the Det Norske Akademis ordbok, the main 'go to' dictionary, as a further example of a regulated language.

Standardisation attempts have been made with the English language, with mixed results at best. Bill Bryson's 'Troublesome Words' or 'Mother Tongue', gives an erudite and wry look at our troublesome language – into which the word 'Yole' should be somewhere near centre stage. 'Yole' is interwoven in our culture as an English homonym[21], or even a homophone[22].

"The term yoal is interesting", Dr Chivers (based in Shetland) writes. "During 16th, 17th, 18th centuries various spellings" [were encountered]. "Basically, the term simply meant a small open boat which could have been four, six or even eight-oared[23]". Although, as boats evolved, so did the names, as appropriate for Shetland – hence a boat with six oars was a sixareen. And interestingly, the favoured contemporary spelling for 'yole', in Shetland, is 'yoal'. In Orkney, the favoured contemporary spelling is 'yole'.

Both Orkney and Shetland dialects have strong leanings to their Scandinavian cousins; many words remain similar - but the word 'yole' is not to be found in Det Norske Akademis ordbok, nor is yoal – I looked. But 'jolle' is. And if I am not mistaken, in Scandinavia 'J' is pronounced as a 'Y' . . . and so onto the 'Jolly Boat' – with 'J' pronounced as in 'jam'. . .

The 'Jolly Boat' conjures a lovely picture of a crew in high spirits, and the air filled with mirth and song. On occasion this must be so,

---

[18] https://en.wikipedia.org/wiki/Acad%C3%A9mie_Fran%C3%A7aise
[19] https://en.wikipedia.org/wiki/Norwegian_Academy
[20] Riksmål - also called Dano-Norwegian, or Bokmål and New Norwegian (Nynorsk) https://www.britannica.com/topic/Norwegian-language
[21] Homonym - same pronunciation and spelling but different meanings
[22] Homophone - same pronunciation but different meaning
[23] Dr Marc Chivers, Director Moder Dy CIC A registered Community Interest Company - SC613493 Bailey Hus, Bridge End, Burra, Shetland ZE2 9LD

grumpy Captains excepted. However, on looking up 'Jolly Boat' in Wikipedia, one reads: "Jolly boats were usually the smallest type of boat carried on ships, and were generally between 16 feet (4.9 m) and 18 feet (5.5 m) long. They were clinker-built and propelled by four or six oars... Jolly boats were used for transporting people and goods to and from shore, for carrying out inspections of the ship, or other small tasks and duties that required only a small number of people, and did not need the use of the larger boats, such as the launch or cutter. Jolly boats were carried on practically all types of warships of the Royal Navy." [24]

The clue is in the word 'jolly' – an Anglicisation of 'jolle'; and, indeed, the Det Norske Akademis ordbok entry for 'jolle' reads:

"jolle on a larger merchant ship and is used, among other things, in connection with maintenance work and painting, jolle for sailboat or yacht, lifeboat or lifeboat. A dinghy was previously most often built of wood, while a newer dinghy can be made of aluminium, plastic"[25]

However, the entry in the 'Språkrådet'- [see the addenda below], is simply a 'small rowing boat...' or a 'lighter sail boat'. And that holds good for both Norwegian languages. So, while 'Språkrådet' is the official 'go to' Norwegian language reference, the Det Norske Akademis ordbok give a much better historical perspective.

There is a similar word in Swedish[26] 'julle'– and the Danish[27] keep 'jolle'.

An interesting project from the Boat Building Academy in Lyme Regis[28] relates how the Smakke Jolle 'Helge', a traditional Danish boat, has been built using plans from a Danish museum. She is a 16' square sailed, double-ended, workboat built entirely in oak. Once completed, commissioner and student Angus Biles will take her to Snekkersten, a former fishing village in the region of Helsingør, in eastern Denmark. The offsets were produced from drawings belonging to Angus, the fit out and rig were based on photos he took in Snekkersten.

The Smakke Jolle Helge

---

[24] https://en.wikipedia.org/wiki/Jolly_boat
[25] https://snl.no/Det_Norske_Akademis_ordbok
[26] Svenska Akademiens Ordbok
[27] https://educalingo.com/en/dic-fr/yole
[28] https://www.boatbuildingacademy.com/boats/16-smakke-jolle-angus-biles/

'Helge' is typical of workboats in many Scandinavian countries, ferrying goods, people and livestock until the early 20th century. Note the last sentence . . . "typical of work boats in many Scandinavian countries ferrying goods, people and livestock."

The stern of the Smakke Jolle Helge

---

[29] Lennart Wallgren

Such was the work of the Orkney yole. So, follow the Danish coast, particularly its Eastern seaboard, along the south and west Swedish coasts, and thence the southern Norwegian coast, and small, beamy, but seaworthy boats abounded throughout. After all, good ideas spread – and while local words and boat build variants exist [e.g., Kostrar or Kosterbåt[29], the snekke, and Skånesnipa], I think, to use the Norwegian/Danish word 'jolle' as the generic term would be acceptable. So, the hypothesis is forming through linguistics – that 'yole' is derived from the word 'jolle'; although that gave rise to the jolly boat, which was the work boat for much larger vessels, and indeed a lifeboat, such was its seaworthiness – as stated above. There is plenty of precedent for this; place names, in particular, outline the movement and settlement of peoples.

So, 'smakke' became 'smack', the smaller sailing vessel, and yawl probably also has its roots in yole [jolle], but now has a distinctive definition in the sailing world [which is beyond the scope of this article] . . .

However, the word 'yole' turns up in French – and it is a waterborne craft; the Académie Française states: "YOLE. n. f.[30]

"Sorte de petit canot léger qui va à la voile et à l'aviron."

Translated as: "A kind of small light boat that sails and can be rowed." Other French dictionaries simply translate 'yole' as 'skiff'. This French yole is a skimpy little thing, grand for exercising, but not the solid work-a-day yole from Orkney. And there is a magnificent

---

[30] http://www.academie-francaise.fr/

sailing yole from Martinique – but again, in a quite different class. Perhaps some person might take this particular project on – the hows and whys of the different applications of the word; 'Vive la difference!'. The 'jolle' is from the Germanic [and, apparently with a hint of Albanian[31]] root of languages, not, it would seem, the Romance. Did the word travel south? But if so, the design that travelled with it is one that we, in the northern climes, would not recognise as a yole.

So, it would seem not unreasonable to suggest that, just as the Orkney word 'fea' comes from 'fjell', or mountain, then, 'yole' is derived from 'jolle', giving, as if needed, further links to Scandinavian boatbuilding traditions.

Addendum:

The Norwegian State official language body is the Språkrådet' or 'The Language Council' (https://www.sprakradet.no/), based at the University of Bergen. They are responsible for compiling the official dictionary https://ordbok.uib.no/ , where you find both bokmål and nynorsk.

Riksmål and Det Norske Akademi do not represent the official Norwegian language; their function is the preservation of the older forms of Norwegian.

---

[31] Norwegian Bokmål Danish Wikipedia

Close up of the clinker strakes (planks) overlapping each other on the bow of our OYA yole Lily. Built by Orkney's only boatbuilder in 2007-8, Ian Richardson.

Papay flit boat, a North Isles yole, heads home from the North Isles ferry SS Thorfinn with a full load. No lifejackets or internal buoyancy in the yole. c.1960s.

Plan form of a typical South Isles yole showing a well rounded boat for buoyancy in Orkney's strong tides and to get across them, home and dry.

Plan form of a Sgoth, Hebrides, another yole variant. The bow is much sharper for cutting through the exposed surf at Neiss' (Ness), with shallow launches and landings.

Two Stroma Yoles in Wick, still used for creel fishing c.2016. The huge beam on Stroma yoles gave much seaworthy buoyancy but made them slow to sail in regattas and lighter winds.

Section 2 Yole uses

[Maurice explores the use of yoles in fishing in both Shetland and Orkney and the changes in the fishing driven by economic circumstances in both archipelagos, expressing his personal views on the politics of the day. He also speculates that the principal driver leading to the current design of the Orkney yole may well have been its use for lobster creeling, which features strongly in Section 3's recollections of life with yoles.]

YOLES FOR FISHING by Maurice Davidson

Shetland

Shetland's population of 20,000 have always relied on fish to live, whilst Orkney's similar sized population, by contrast, has relied mainly on farming. This is because Orkney has an easier soil to farm, derived from the sediments of Lake Orcadie under the Ice Age, compared to the rough volcanic rock of Shetland. Good boating conditions are seen in Shetland's long, sheltered voes, with short crossings between mainly large, long islands and less tidal waters, further from the big obstruction to sea tides provided by mainland Britain.[xxxii]

Shetland's sharp, sleek Norway yoles, or yoals as they call them, are fine, fast boats to row out a few miles to fish, with a single mast and small square sail to drive the heavier laden yole home. Yoals, and quills (pronounced whills) in Orkney, were narrow, fast rowing boats, well suited for nearshore handline fishing and for driving caaing whales (smaller pilot whales) by the score onto the shore each year. The latter activity is the more common, the further north you go from Shetland to the Faroes, Iceland and the Lofoten islands.

Larger, six- to seven-metre Shetland yoals, or fowereens for four rowers, still only 1.2 metres wide, easy and cheap to build locally, were initially owned by the lairds, who usually took the major share of any catch in payment for their use. Lairds also loaned lines and hooks to their men and put them further in debt, on record as charging 20% interest – which made them the payday loan sharks of their day. All the burden of risk was on the poor crofters. The rich got richer, sitting comfortably in front of their warm fireplace, with a glass of port.[xli]

As inner coasts were overfished, Shetland's lairds were concerned that larger Dutch busses and English smacks were raiding the larger offshore cod and ling. So, Shetlands' lairds built larger yoals, sixareens, up 8 metres long, 2.5 metres wide but with only 0.75 metres draught. These were more seaworthy rowing boats, to pull out the ten to thirty miles to yet deeper and bigger fish, and pay off the laird's investment. The skilful fisher/crofters had to fish for one or even two nights in open sixareens, laying and hauling up to 6,000 fathoms or 10 kilometres of baited gret lines[32] twice a day.

---

[32] Long lines of baited hooks

Wick harbour 1865, eight hundred open clinker Moray, Scaffie and Fifie yaals up to 10M long, unloading herring. These huge yoles, which maximise buoyancy, greatly influenced Orkney Yole design.

They would then hoist a single dipping lugsail and sail back to their laird's crude stone and turf shelters. These were normally on a desolate exposed stony beach, as near as possible to the fishing grounds, to save time. Many drownings happened, not far out at sea on the long swells, but near to land, in shallow, more tidal sea where surf breaks easily and when the crew was cold, wet and tired.

As folk had to fish further and further offshore for longer periods, open sixareens were inevitably caught out and swamped, being heavily laden with ling and cod. Many families lost their husbands, fathers and brothers, especially in the early gales of the desperate 1860s – 1880s. There was no romance of the sea in these sleek yoals, just crofters desperate to feed their families caught in the laird's debt slavery for life.[xli]

The Haaf[33] fishery, as Shetlanders called it, developed in the 1830s going up to 40 miles offshore, to compete with larger open sailing scaffies and fifies from the wealthier east of Scotland. It was a gamble by the Shetland lairds, who risked a minimum of capital in cheap, open boats that ensured maximum risk for crofters, who had to man them in the cold, wet and miserable conditions. As such, the sixareens' haaf fishing was largely finished by the 1880s, when larger, decked, east coast boats proved to be much better sea boats in the gales. After that, industrial, steam-powered trawlers caught all the inshore and offshore fish.

Orkney

Orkney's first Earl Stewart banned the import of all Norraway yols in 1525. This ensured he retained a complete monopoly on Orkney's and Shetland's cod fishery and all the cash that local fishermen were getting in their hand, from visiting Dutch fish traders. Tax avoidance is nothing new! [xxxii]

The second "Black Pate", Earl Patrick Stewart the tyrant, did the same in 1582, and then taxed all gret line fishing for cod, to control sales of fish to Hanseatic merchant ships from the Baltic. In Orkney, these gin-bearing smacks were popular with fishermen in the east, in South Ronaldsay, Burray and Walls, until war restricted the availability of gin, in the 1700s. North Ronaldsay was also famous for salt cod, as the Traill family there forced men out to sea in the laird's small yoles, to earn cash in hand, and tax-free liquor.[xxx]

After Earl Patrick Stewart was hanged in 1615, cod fishing flourished again all over Orkney. But this time the lairds closely controlled the trade, renting all boats and gear to their poor crofters to fish with, for them. After the Jacobite Rising of 1745 in Scotland, English-leaning earls and lairds took over the land, clearing crofters off the best land, making them dig heather and drain wet bogs for new land. They also sent men out to sea to fish in their small yoles, the catch to be sold to the new industrial cities south. [xxxi]

---

[33] Deep sea

Cod fishing with the South Isles yole Gremsa off the Old Man of Hoy on a very languid sea.
Yoles are normally used for sailing nowadays.

If anyone complained, the laird's appointed minister would kindly tell the family how good it was that the laird had given them all land and houses and work and boats and hooks. They should get out to sea and fish for the laird or be judged even more harshly in the next world!

Brims, Rackwick, Whaness in Hoy, Sanday's fishing terraces, Westray's shore crofts, Rousay's Sourin cotts and more, were all settlements occupied by poor crofters evicted from their better old croft lands by the new Scots lairds. There was no romantic crofters' life to be had here.[xlii]

However, Orkney's good farming soil saved its crofters from all being forced out to sea in small 4.5 metre yoles, by greedy lairds. But its coastal seas were also full of fish, feeding on deep water nutrients and plankton from the Atlantic, stirred up by strong tidal streams.

A government war bounty for Scottish cured fish in 1727 encouraged the lairds to send more yoles out to sea. More yoles were built to cope with this increased demand, as the huge numbers of nousts[34] along lairds' shorelines still bear witness to. Such nousts kept yoles handy for fishing at all times, even at the Hall o' Klestran's[35] large noust. [xxx]

In the late 1700s, the lairds forced our ancestors out onto the hill land, clearing their heather and sowing seed. Then later in July and into autumn, the women were forced out on the beaches, clearing and burning all the ware[36] in large stone pots, which are still to be found on some isolated shorefaces. The French Revolutionary and Napoleonic Wars cut off supplies of glass chemicals and suddenly Orkney ware was worth a lot, for its potash and soda residue. However, collection and processing was heavy and poisonous work.

The Napoleonic war made fish more expensive, as southern seas became out of bounds. So, as the women toiled onshore, the men were forced out to sea, also to make more money for the laird. They fished in the laird's boats, using his fishing gear – all loaned at high rates of interest, so if gear was lost the laird made even more from the sale of replacements.[xxx]

Initially, in the 1760s, cod was caught by handlining with sprols[37]. But soon inshore seas were cleared of fish in the greed for more. Gret lines, some 3 or 4 miles long, were loaned, and set deeper and further offshore, until it became unsafe for the Orcadian small yoles out overnight, over-heavy with gear and cod. In November 1738, 14 Graemsay men were lost fishing and sealing for the laird on Sule Skerry, in a desperate gamble at that time of the year, even for a couple of 6-metre gret yoles. They left 63 widows and orphans.

LOW'S HISTORY OF ORKNEY in 1780, contains the following references to the sea by this Orkney minister:

---

[34] A boat haul, a shallow depression where Orkney yoles were overwintered
[35] Hall of Clestrain (childhood home of renowned Arctic explorer Dr. John Rae)
[36] Seaweed or kelp
[37] A hand line split into two lines using a metal bow

John Folster's quill, a smaller, slender yole type rowing boat. Light and cheap for hauling up beaches every night. Yoles developed to safely carry more creels and fish. c1930.

"Fishing, supplies present necessity of that with fish of the most ordinary kinds, it is only prosecuted as far as poverty and want of the inhabitants force them from day to day to seek in the sea an addition to the scant subsistence which the land affords them.

Imports, spirits, tobacco, tea, coffee, silks, velvets…

Exports, a little grain, a little beef, butter, oil…calf and rabbit skins, feathers….. but the staple commodity of the county is kelp …brings in a large profit to the proprietors".

"A century ago in 1680s there was a very considerable fishery, which no doubt was much in Orkney's favour…. we are like people starving in the midst of plenty.

Husbandry is at a stand and makes no progress account of racked rents and short leases…..I can see nothing for it but the inhabitants of these isles….must leave house and home."

"Dutch fleets cover all the fishing grounds of these seas from the Moray Firth to the Shetlands…60,000 lobsters are caught a year in the South Isles and sent to London on their well smacks."

As fish prices increased with war, the government cancelled all subsidies for larger smacks heading out to sea. Local yoles all over the east coast could then compete for fish and make a good profit for their owners, firstly lairds, then (by the 1820s) the fish merchants.[xxxiv]

Large open Moray yoles came to Orkney first to fish, before going on to Shetland, and soon cleared the sheltered east side by 1800. Boom and bust economy yet again. But the fast tides of the Pentland Firth and the cod bounty (£3 per ton of salted and dried cod) kept cod fishing alive until the wars ended in 1815, after which all subsidy vanished. Rackwick and Walls on Hoy became famous for producing tens of thousands of peat-smoked, salt cod.[xxx]

Fish merchants from the Moray and Aberdeen coasts set up on eastern ports of Orkney in Whitehall, Kettletoft, Burray and the Hope. Here they gave loans for boats and lines and paid better prices for the salt cod (and herring) than those paid under the lairds' monopoly. Traders also made money from the crofters, but Orcadians now had a chance of finally owning their own yole and making enough money to rid themselves of generations-old debt due to their lairds.

The Government's Washington Report, in 1849, recommended that all offshore fishing boats be decked and have a deep keel, but Scottish wealthy landlords refused to comply. The more practical, southern fish merchants went ahead and incurred the expense, as they wanted to land their fish ashore rather than have it left at sea with their boats and men in rough weather. This happened all too often in the mid-1800s, when fishermen had to sail further offshore.[xxxi]

By 1860, Orkney had over 700 yoles, some over seven metres long, fishing locally and employing nearly 3,000 fishermen for lobsters, cod and herring and landing some 500 tons of fish a year.

We have a lot to thank wars for in Orkney, from Napoleon onwards! Without them all the big changes for good - jobs, money and ideas from South - would never have come here. Oil could be the rare exception, so long as an oily disaster is avoided in Scapa Flow.

Small lug sail and spreet sail yoles sailing into Skippie Geo, Birsay after a day's fishing. All yoles had to be hauled out above the high water line every day as there is no sheltered mooring here.

Like in Shetland, the 15-20 metre decked scaffies and fifies – Firthies and Zulus - both larger, modern developments of their yoles, or yaals as Wick folk would say, finally fished and netted Orkney's inshore waters clean of the former huge shoals of cod. These were safer and more seaworthy boats.

Orkney's lairds also put some money into herring boats. These were mainly older, large open Moray scaffies going cheap, as decked boats took over in the south, following horrendous loss of life in the offshore storms of 1860s and 1880s. But these old, huge, eight- or even ten-metre, open clinker boats had been built for east coast piers, not for beach hauls, so must have been unwieldy round Orkney's tidal isles. However, the general depression of the late 1880s then forced a huge downturn in fishing and farming.

Finally, the 1890s recession took hold, farm and fish prices fell and these great boats were cut in two and upended and turned into hen houses, while the more seaworthy southern competition dominated. Fish subsidies were handed out in the 1897 recession, and a surge in boatbuilding followed again, for those who could afford it.[xxx] 4,000 Orcadians emigrated in the 1890s, impoverished by wars in Europe and short-term lairds' profiteering.[xxx]

Lapsters (Lobsters) and Partans (edible brown crabs)

Probably the main influence on Norway yoles curving further out into our unique Orkney yoles must be the huge numbers of shellfish found crawling on the faster tides here. More lobsters and, since World War II, partans are found and caught round Orkney than maybe anywhere else in the world, for a comparable area.

The key to the abundance of shellfish in Orkney waters must be the strong tides squeezing round the north of Scotland. Maybe food is carried in, or shellfish just catch a ride as they migrate from the Atlantic to the North Sea, so they are more concentrated in our tidal squeeze point. Certainly, Shetland and Caithness have nothing like the numbers found round Orkney's shores.

Records going back before Low's book in 1780 also show that South Isles yoles were fishing then for lobsters in commercial numbers for big well smacks, sailing up from London. These valuable delicacies were carried south alive to their lordships' tables. 60,000 may be an exaggeration by Low, but undoubtedly this was a major fishery, even then. Again, in the 1770s, 1850s and 1900s, records show the existence of an extensive lobster fishery.

Initially, the lobsters were shore-caught or caught using small yoles and heavy, baited net rings, left for a tide on the seabed and hauled quickly up by hand, trapping the blue warriors.[xxxi] My uncles still practised this manual fishing using a flattie, when they were youngsters, after World War I in Graemsay. It was a great incentive to learn to swim, since hauling the heavy hoop in on the side of a small flattie could easily roll the boat over. And the lobsters in those early days were all enormous, according to a rose-eyed, and aging, uncle James.

Inkwell creels on large Yorkshire cod boats in the Napoleonic wars were copied by local fishermen, but were easily damaged and heavy to haul.

Fishing below the 380M vertical cliffs off the Head of Hoy. Jan towing a line for lythe in the sheltered sea, on the South Isles yole Gremsa, having sailed five miles from Stromness.

Catches increased to over 100,000 lobsters by 1834. My uncle James even invented hauling these creels from the ends, not the top as with inkwells, to reduce drag. This is a style still commonly used today.

The problem for fishermen in creeling yoles was that they had to carry these bulky and heavy iron ring nets, then creels, out to sea, shift them every day, and needed more room to stack them. Norway yoles changed to Orkney yoles, 1.2 metres wide stretched to 2.2 metres wide, and even a 3-metre beam on the larger yoles in the Pentland Firth, where catches of lobsters were, and are still, bigger than elsewhere in Orkney. Side decks became common to set creels on in wider boats. So, the key reason why we have the Orkney yole in its current shape may well be that it was designed for lobsters, which earned ready cash to pay for boats, gear and the rent.

The halcyon days of lobster fishing were during World War II. Fishing was restricted but crofting yoles still creeled in Scapa Flow. Lobsters were plentiful, even crawling up the mooring ropes. Large ones sat on top of creels, telling younger ones inside the bits of bait they wanted, too big to get in the door. They were sold in huge numbers direct to Royal Navy officers on warships in Scapa Flow as fishermen realised just how much more they could get by selling direct rather than through the Kirkwall fish merchants. Untaxed pound notes were stuffed into the crofters' waders' piggybank.

Many a Ferguson tractor was bought on the back of a lobster! I couldn't have afforded to go to university without our summer lobster fishing.

Stromness fishermen did the same and promptly formed the famous Orkney Fishermen's Society cooperative, soon after World War II. It is still very strong and active today. Rousay, Sanday, Stronsay and Westray also formed their local isles' shellfish co-operatives, but only Westray's remains.

20 creels piled up in uncle James's 5.5-metre yole, in the choppy September seas, as we brought them in for the winter, were a handful. Fishing yoles typically had some 100 single buoyed creels, expensive to build in winter and not to be wasted.

Creel haulers linked to engines, built locally by blacksmiths like Willie Mowatt in Burwick, could soon haul hundreds of creels from yet deeper water, on long bush ropes, ten at a time, but these needed yet larger eight-metre yoles, with a three-metre beam, with heavier diesel engines. Such a size was now practical for Orkney, as there were good concrete piers to tie up to. Small wooden luggie boxes, floating next to moorings, gave way to huge concrete lobster pond stores, to hold lobsters until they could be flown off for a better price.

Nowadays 11-metre fishing boats haul 300 – 500 creels every two days on long bush ropes, to make fishing pay. Such numbers are well beyond the capacity of a small yole.

Partans, which we used to eat or throw back, have found a huge market in China, along with the lobsters. With some 12,000 creels on larger industrial, offshore partan boats now, it cannot be long before these are overfished and the supply dries up.

Fishermen at Rackwick, Hoy hauling their standard 18 foot South Isles yole up their rugged shore.
Slightly posed for the camera with cod and halibut on show. c1910.

[Maurice's second article in this section explores the many uses of our Orkney yole other than fishing, with insights drawn from the tales of locals, in and around Scapa Flow. There seems to have been a particular penchant for throwing green bottles of home brew overboard amongst the sources of these tales!]

OTHER USES FOR YOLES by Maurice Davidson

As well as catching lobsters for cash and handline fishing, yoles were also used for the transport of crofters, livestock, fertiliser, food, feed and equipment on and off the isles.

Every year, isles that had no peat - such as North Ronaldsay, Faray, Sanday and Graemsay - had annual "holidays" in the spring and autumn, for yoles to sail over to neighbouring peaty Eday and Rysa to cut, dry and load peats back. It took days of hard and heavy labour, to cut enough fuel for cooking and for heat to last through winter. It was an essential job for wide, stable yoles to carry home the peat, usually laden to the gunwales, after the crew had had a few bottles of home brew to ease the backache.

As the wind got up, the crew's job was to move peat over to windward or to lighten the load and throw peat overboard, a hard move to do after all that work. A regular brown trail was often seen between Rysa and Graemsay, and a few green bottles, too.

Yoles are very seaworthy open boats and were often used to row out to ships wrecked round Orkney's shores, even in wild and chaotic seas. Local knowledge of where the quieter seas would be was essential.

When the *Albion*, a large full-rigged ship, crashed ashore on New Year's Day 1866, in heavy seas at the West Light off Graemsay, all 43 emigrant passengers heading for New York, along with 24 crew, were taken off at great risk by local yoles. Unfortunately, one yole was capsized by the Royal Mail steamer's paddlewheel and ten people were drowned. But to save 61 people as the ship broke up on the rocks - there was no ship left the next day - was a huge testament to the characteristics of small yoles and their skilled crews in those breaking seas.[xliii]

In December 1908, five Faray men rowed their small 4-metre skiff off the nearby Holm in a wild storm to rescue eight trawlermen. Two runs were needed and everyone was saved, proving that small open boats can be just as seaworthy as larger ships, in skilled hands.[xliii]

Trips to the town, Kirkwall or Stromness, were the highlight of most months, away from the drudgery of croft work. Yoles made it possible to sell eggs, buy food or drink not available in the isles, visit folk, gossip and have a laugh. Once or twice a year, their sheep or small cattle would be loaded, with care, onto strengthened floorboards or towed behind in heavy cow boats, and carried to the mart for sale. Inevitably, this needed a communal effort to get animals on and off rock jetties and became a communal celebration in the hotel after the sale. Two or three yoles would sail together to help each other out, as when things got out of hand, there was safety in numbers. Cattle were sometimes given tobacco to keep them quiet on the yole, but frequently some lively cow would jump overboard and have to be tied on to the back of the yole and swim to town.

Small but wide Sanday-built North Isles flit boat of the late 1960s, full of folk's messages (shopping) from the Toon (Kirkwall), motoring from the SS Sigurd to Papay, as no deep water pier.

There were no regular ferries to the isles until after World War I, and even then yoles rowed passengers, cargo and towed cattle out, to be slung onto the waiting steamer. You had to be quick off the mark on the yole as cattle, with a canvas sling squeezing their belly, would scatter excrement over everyone as they spun around above you.

One of the highlights of my mother's youth was being carried on old Johna Gray's back from rocks to the yole - he only fell twice! She got away with just one ankle wet. He was a real gentleman!

These slow and unreliable steamers carried on till after World War II. Then the Council built concrete piers on most isles and employed faster ferries to Kirkwall and Stromness, in an attempt to stop wholesale abandonment of the North and South Isles.

People had got used to getting regular cash in hand from the thousands of armed forces stationed in Orkney, for fresh hens, eggs, cheese and lobsters. They also got used to the city-style life which the forces brought with them, with cinemas, bands and regular dances.

When the 30,000 troops were all gone, plus 60,000 sailors on the warships, the Orkney isles were empty, and poor again. No one wanted to return to the old hard way of life under the lairds, so they voted with their feet and emigrated by the thousands to Australia, New Zealand and Canada, or even just to Kirkwall.

Orkney's population, especially in the Isles, declined by 15,000, in just over a hundred years, from 32,225 in 1861 to 17,077 in 1971. It was a depressing time here, forgotten and left to rot by central governments. Isles populations shrank by 65% or more, until the Labour Government's Highlands and Islands Development Board grants injected new hope into fishing and farming. Then, by the mid-1970s, oil arrived at Flotta, and finally roll-on roll-off car ferries gave easier access to the towns and supermarkets.[xxx]

With regular ferries, good piers and frozen fish fingers, by the 1960s yoles were history. They were still launched for annual sailing regattas, but often slowly left to rot in their noust[38] by the shore. With more farm machines and fewer people on larger farms, the isles' culture changed to the tune of television and buying everything in. Faster car ferries link us ever closer to the supermarket chain.

But our social needs have not been dampened, we still need to meet and do things together, to celebrate and commiserate and get on with community life. The Orkney Yole Association was formed in 2000, as only one yole was sailed regularly in Stromness in the late 1990s, with a few more at Westray and Longhope regattas.

There are now ten sailing South Isles yoles in Stromness and Longhope, twelve North Isles skiffs and yoles in Westray and three lugsail yoles from Papay. They are all enthusiastically sailed and raced and argued over, at regattas and weekly social races. Young folk still thrill to their liveliness, over the tides and waves among Orkney's isles. Long may it last.

---

[38] A boat haul, a shallow depression in the shore face, where Orkney yoles were overwintered

The Rousay post boat, a small North Isles lugsail yole, crossing the Eynhallow Sound in a gale c.1890.
Two ferries were swamped here with loss of life in the 1880s.

Hoy's strengthened North Isles yole flit boat tows a cow out to meet the Hoy Head ferry, along with passengers in the yole. A single dipping lugsail mast and oars power the yole. Seageo c1920.

Fishermen at Windwick, South Ronaldsay land a good size halibut from their gretlines set in the tide 3 miles offshore. Their yoles can be seen on the shore before being hauled up.

A Graemsay yole tows the large Graemsay Coo Boat to Stromness (ex German Navy teak pinnace saved from the Royal Navy), converted with removable side for loading kye (cattle) c1952.

Large Orkney Yole (York Boat), 43' long replica, built by Orcadian joiners, Isbister Bros. in the Hudsons Bay Co, to run furs and stores hundreds of miles into the Canadian forests.

Section 3 Recollections of life with yoles

[This first article contains a couple of stories from John Budge, a long serving Lifeboatman and farmer, as recorded by Ron Bulmer. John is a terrific raconteur, musician and a repository for many a fine story in the best local tradition of Hoy's oral history.]

SALUTARY TALES FROM HOY – as told by John Budge

After Mainland Orkney, Hoy is the biggest island in the archipelago, and probably still maintains the largest fleet of yoles in Orkney, though sadly not all are now seaworthy.

A number of folk were approached for tales, just the mundane, everyday story would have been fine. Tales of derring-do must exist, but this is a modest community. I suspect such stories are a matter of fact and not worthy of note – let us never forget that some 50 years ago the Longhope lifeboat went down with all hands. Within a year a new crew was trained up and ready for that call.

So, to glean a couple of tales from a former RNLI mechanic is entirely appropriate – a man born, raised, and farmed on Hoy[39] – is an almost unimpeachable source. Yet modest enough to admit he never sailed and knows nothing about the art of sailing – though, as a Lifeboatman there is the marvellous assumption that he [or she!] could manage any boat. . . I hope I haven't shattered an illusion here!

Perhaps it is by no small coincidence that two senior members of the current Longhope Lifeboat own two iconic yoles, the *Mohican* and *Family Pride*. Hopefully both will remain seaworthy for a good many years yet – but there are very many others who lived and worked on Hoy and would have been yole owners as a matter of course.

Mohican laid up at Longhope. Photo by Ron Bulmer

So, this is a sad story of the loss of two men, in the early part of the 20th century. These are the sort of stories that make for folklore, but remain salutary none-the-less, even if the events took place in

---

[39] Actually, South Walls. Hoy [island of] is split into three parishes, North and South Walls, and Hoy – though strictly Hoy and Graemsay.

relatively contemporary times. After all it wasn't until 1989 that the Marine Accident Investigation Branch (MAIB) was established, with their detailed investigative discipline and a drive for the truth.

The story unfolds in the Bay of Quoys, which gives fair shelter, but at low tide, the bay can, especially at low spring tides, become a beautiful expanse of sand. People have tried to keep a boat in the bay, but to have any sort of shelter, the mooring would dry out. To access a boat, one would have to wait for sufficient water to row out to the larger vessel. The two hapless men, it would seem, got into a dinghy [a flattie[40] perhaps?], which then sheared off, and caught the yole in the quarter. Such was the force of the smaller boat that it sheared the yole into two, drowning both men; the Nicolson brothers from Braebister had met their untimely end.

A sad tale indeed, as on certain points of the tide, there would have been sufficient water to keep the boat afloat, yet shallow enough to wade to safety. Though that detail is now lost. Had they been trapped in the wreckage? Rendered unconscious from a blow on the head? Or suffered with the almost immediate effect of cold-water shock? Few could swim in those days, and the wearing of lifejackets virtually never happened.

Overlooking the bay is the farm of Garson, which has view of the entire sweep of the Bay O' Quoys. A woman who lived there, only some two days previously had a premonition. I can't say whether she had 'second sight'; but, she saw, quite clearly, men with ropes running along the shoreline.

And, on the day, men could be seen running, with ropes in a forlorn attempt to save the Nicolson boys. . . could it have been a 'flan'? A Hoy word, describing the vicious whirl wind of water, that can whip the sea into a frenzy? A particularly vicious 'flan' can put water over the island of Graemsay.

The boys lay at rest, in the little kirkyard overlooking the Bay of Creekland.

The next yarn is not cheery either.

Three boys[41], on their way home from Stromness to Longhope, decided to call into the now long-gone inn at North Ness. Was drink involved? Could it be that their spirit of immortality was already fuelled from a social activity in Stromness? Then the time came to make their way [probably erratically] back into the usually sheltered confines of North Bay. When, seeing the welcome lights of the well-known hostelry filled with their friends and neighbours, they decided to have 'one more'? But this is conjecture, mere supposition; at that time not even the Ayre had been built linking South Walls permanently to the rest of the Island of Hoy. . . so, pre-1912. Up until then, access to south Walls was over a sand bar at low tide, or least off high tide.

---

[40] A flattie is a small rowing boat with flat hull, that could be cheaply and easily built, but was a robust and solid craft.

[41] Boys can refer to any male of any age

On the following morning, to horrified onlookers, a yole was found lying on its side, the mast on the water. The only person who could be seen was Tom Gunn, clinging desperately to the side.

He was retrieved, I'd imagine badly shaken, and hypothermic, but his two compatriots did not survive. When Tom Gunn was given an examination, he had split the sole of his leather boot. In his effort for survival, he'd used the nile[42] pin for slim purchase, and had pressed so solidly down that the nile pin had not just split his boot, but had gone right into his foot.

It must be said that Tom Gunn was no stranger to the wild vagaries of that particular sea. He was the Fronts man of the Longhope Lifeboat – boats offering little or no shelter, and anybody up in the bow would likely be first to get a salty drenching. Indeed, direct descendants of his still crew the £2.5 million Longhope Lifeboat, which still doesn't diminish the hazardous nature of their work.

Miscalculation? Bad luck? Human frailty and error? We'll never know. This was all long before the MAIB. But what does remain, is that yoles are well suited to Orkney waters. They were the taxi of the day; they carried peats from islands like Rysa Little back to Hoy, the deceased from Fara to Flotta, Fara having no Kirk yard [cemetery], and were used as 'flit' boats, for house removals; yoles were a vital link to a scattered archipelago; and as in this world of fast, safe, reliable travel, accidents can and do happen.

2017, haunting remnants of flatties and dinghies in South Ronaldsay's once busy noust at Sandside. A sheltered bay with ready access to the Flow and Pentland Firth.

---

[42] A nile is the bung for the drain hole where water drains when a boat is laid up over the winter

Sailing on a good day with a large group of young folk returning from Hoy Sound on the three sailed yole Gremsa. It is not always rough in this very tidal area.

[Another raconteur from Hoy meets Ron and tells yet another tale of weather playing havoc with what should have been a routine trip by yole from Stromness to Hoy….]

HOY SOUND MEETS TERRY – Terry Thompson tells a tale to Ron Bulmer

It's always a pleasure to sit in Terry and Jean's comfortable front room. Tea and biscuits are the norm [and on occasion a stronger libation], but it's the yarns, all true – naturally, that give the real pleasure. Though somehow they are all slightly larger than life – but don't ever doubt their veracity. Even their house itself, The Bu, which translates as the 'principal farm', sits tucked, not just into the landscape, but is part of the landscape. The records go back to the 12th century. And Terry, of course, had a tale.

He bought a yole. For £50. The seller would have been happy to give it away. But this was not Terry's way of doing things, even though, to be fair, the yole was in need of repair. So, albeit reluctantly on the now vendor's part, the purchase was made, and the deal done.

The boat, indeed, was barely useable. However, as Terry, himself, said, when he worked south[43], Orcadian ingenuity was much prized.

'If we had a pallet', said the South country Boy, 'we'd probably just burn it. But not you Orcadians, you'd turn it into one o' them yoles … wish we could do that.'

So it was, that this much prized ingenuity saw some deft working with fibre glass paste moulded into the seemingly hopeless and irreparable crack. The job was then bound even more tightly with the judicious application of some coach bolts. To finish the repair, the work was sanded smooth and painted. Sadly, I never saw the boat, but my guess is, that repair and original would be indistinguishable.

Best of all, the boat was 'dry'. Some boats are 'dry', and others are 'wet'. With natural materials, a 'dry boat', will absorb little, if any, water into the bilges. A 'wet boat' can require constant pumping.

Now fitted with a suitably smart 5hp outboard, Terry was cajoled into getting a sailing rig – but it was one of those things that never quite happened. Be that as it may, this yole fared well on the water, and just as well as events turn out.

* * *

The time came to go home, back to Hoy, across Hoy Sound. Perhaps not as notorious as the Pentland Firth – nevertheless this is a small arm of the Atlantic. Next point west is the north Labrador coast, Canada.

The weather was fine, ne'er a ripple in the sheltered harbour of Stromness. However, the long-term skipper of the Hoy ferry, Stevie Mowat, nodded towards Hoy – behind the large lump that's Ward Hill, Orkney's highest upland – loomed an ominous black cloud.

---

[43] '…south' Anywhere south of Orkney.

South Isles Yole Gremsa running before a good breeze from Graemsay into Hoy Sound on a fair day in 2021, with Jan, Bill (89 years and still enjoying it) and Flo on her third sail.

Yet, nothing gave an indication of what was to come. Terry looked at Stevie: 'Well' he said 'Time I was away', and cast off into the sparkling flat calm waters, looking forward to a fine tea.

So, wind against tide. For those not in the know, this is when two elemental forces go in opposite directions. Wind one way, tide the other. Combined with the unfettered ocean suddenly being squeezed into a gap a couple of miles wide, the effects can be, shall we say, interesting?

Terry certainly did find it interesting, as to his horror, the ominous cloud heralded a change for the worse; strong winds funnelled into a fury by Hoy's valleys, with an outgoing tide, the conditions were less than favourable . . . the swell mounted and grew, hiding the small boat from view; Stevie Mowat later confided that, if Terry had needed rescuing, the size of swell was such that retrieval would have been out of the question. . .

But as a growing boy, Terry had a good teacher. 'Keep your ballast back', Willie Groat, an old hand of the old school, advised. 'You'll don't need to let your boat plough into the waves, but skirt ower the top.'

And indeed, Terry's ballast was well back, all 56 pounds of it; and so was he – now at the point when the idea of wearing a life jacket greatly appealed. And there it was, safely secured on the for'ard thwart. With the state of the sea, and trim of the boat, Terry had to keep the weight well back. Preservation kept him rooted. If only, if only, he'd slipped the life jacket on before leaving Stromness.

But other things were in Terry's favour. Those days of his immortal and indestructible youth, when one never considered life jackets, or spares, and creeping out into the Pentland Firth, learning about boats, tides, wind and weather had been a useful proving ground. Local boats in home waters gives one a margin for error, that might not otherwise be the case.

The little outboard kept the speed down allowing the boat to ride over the waves, and the bellied sides carved a way through the waves. To be lost in a wall of heaving water is not a good place. So, not only was Stevie Mowat's watch one of concern, but so too was Nigel's – one of Terry's boys. Knowing how poor the conditions had become, Nigel had left the house, and looked over Hoy Sound, but saw nothing. The small yole was dwarfed by the towering and confused sea; any hope that the onlookers might have had of catching sight to ensure that all was well, was dashed.

It can be a long wait at such times. . .

In the sheltered and comforting bay just below the house is a spit of sand. Home; the quiet grind of sand on the keel. Terry's words on reaching safety were never recorded. Probably, unlikely to be repeatable.

To navigate in such conditions took skill and nerve. But his days of keeping a yole were done. The little boat was sold, and went back to Stromness, under tow.

* * *

2012, South Isles yole Gremsa sailing into the new Hoy marina, built by Jimmie Moar and friends by hand digging out the deep Whaness Burn.

There is a postscript to this – in the bar of the Stroma Bank Hotel, Terry was relating his tale to the then RNLI Coxswain of the Longhope Lifeboat – who not unnaturally knew these waters well, and it being a small community, knew Terry.

Now, to digress slightly, remember when learning to drive, with the instruction 'Easy on the throttle' – and I don't think Terry would mind me saying – but this particular instruction never really bothered him too much.

So, the Coxswain was reassured that Terry had such a small 5hp outboard . . . 'I know you' he said. 'A bigger engine and you'd have opened her up, and driven through the waves, and not neatly over them'.

Terry put his beer down, gently, on the bar. 'Oh, no, not today I wouldn't, I can assure you of that'.

Ian Richardson's three sailed yole Frances goose-winged, running before the wind in Stromness harbour, 2005.

1888, Mr Mowat, Linksness ran Hoy's first postboat to Stromness across Burra and Hoy Sound's tide races. Oars not recommended. The standard, easily handled, three sailed rig is seen.

[This next article takes us a little further back in time to around 1890 and across to Hoy. None of us editors can imagine rowing 60 miles over two days in a yole - or using stone anchors. Clearly folk then were much tougher than today. But regatta mishaps sound very familiar!]

MEMORIES OF HOY – Sailing Experiences of Fifty Years ago by G.L. Thomson, from a talk at a Stromness Sailing Club social

Reproduced from The Orcadian, 29 March 1939

In the old days everyone in Hoy had to learn to handle a small boat, as there was no other means of transport between the islands. Almost every householder had one or two boats, and Stromness was visited more often than it is today. Up till the time the *Saga* was built, the mails to Hoy and Graemsay were carried by a small yawl from Hoy, and as there was no parcel post or postcards, one could have carried the total mail for Hoy in a lady's handbag.

There was no house-to-house delivery in those days either. When the post-boat arrived, we went to the Post Office after school hours and waited for the letters. No combination of shop and Post Office then – the kitchen table was used as counter, and we had to wait till the letters were looked over and handed to the owners, or to anyone who would deliver them on their way home. Whaness was then a new colony, and only those who were too old or too young and the women-folks remained at home during the summer.

At the house next to ours there lived an old man called Robbie, who was my early tutor in sailing and fishing. He had a small yawl which he used for fishing between Hoy and Graemsay, and on Saturdays or during the holidays he often took me with him. Strong and treacherous tides made inshore fishing a fine art. It was only possible with high and low water slack, and the tide Robbie liked was when it was high water between 11am and 1pm. We went off an hour before high water and fished at the edge of the tide. Very often a Graemsay boat or two would come and fish on their own side. The Graemsay men seldom crossed to our side of the tide, but if they did, my skipper did not look on them with favour, and often forcibly said so.

No need for "Keep-fit" class

When the tide slackened, the middle of the Sound was common property. Owing to the rocky bottom, we used a stone as anchor, and it was my duty to put out this stone and haul it in again. You will understand it was not an easy job, and the less shifting the better for me. At certain times of the year cod were plentiful, and Robbie used to be able to keep this district supplied with fish, while the larger ones were split and cured. As the fishing ground was near, we often rowed to the marks, the sail being mostly used for coming before the wind. Rowing was more in favour then than now.

Old Robbie used to tell of how once he went with Peter Young, who lived in Hoy and whose wife lived at Staxigoe, Caithness. They rowed a small yawl all the way there. After beaching the boat, they made their way up to the cottage where Peter's wife lived.

South Isles sailing yoles moored in Stromness' sheltered harbour, piled high with lobster creels, to set out West. The North boat steamer at the pier carries cattle to Aberdeen. c1905.

But Peter walked with a limp, and his wife saw them coming and, recognizing her husband, she fled to the nearest house, leaving the tea things on the table.

When the men came to the house, they found the lady gone but, in no way daunted, they had their tea and when bedtime came, retired. In the morning they made their breakfast and went back to their boat, took an oar each, and rowed back to Creckland[44] in Hoy, none the worse of their two days' row of about 60 miles. No need of a "keep-fit" class for these men!

Old Robbie had many clients in the West Mainland as well as in the South Isles. I remember crossing over to Stromness to the Market, and as the herring boats had not arrived home, there was no one to take charge of the boat but Robbie. He was very anxious to get to the market, and persuaded my mother and two of us schoolboys to come with him.

It was a lovely day, and I have no remembrance of how we got to Stromness. We tied the boat up at Brass's Pier. When time for going home came Robbie arrived, being armed down the slipway by two well-known Outertown friends, and feeing very happy. They helped him into the boat, but Robbie was afraid to trust himself on a thwart, so he sat down in the bottom of the boat and sang psalms. My mother steered, and we got the sails set, and went home, west-about, in company with a Graemsay boat, without anyone knowing that our skipper had lapsed.

Bait Flowing down the tide

Robbie's greatest difficulty was in getting bait. He was then about 80 years of age, and we often went for lug and limpets for him. There was a young lady from Wick on holiday at our house. She watched the old man go off in his boat to the fishing, and saw him return with his fish. She told him she would like to accompany him some time, so it was arranged that she would do so on the first fine day. Robbie spent a laborious evening getting bait, and next forenoon Miss Hanson set sail with him. After arriving at the marks and getting his boat moored, the first thing Robbie had to do was to bail the boat, as she was very leaky. The water was over the bailing tin, and Robbie lifted a tin-full of water and emptied it over the side. To his dismay he saw the hard-gathered bait floating down the tide. The young lady said his remarks were strong and to the point. As he had no more bait, he hauled in his anchor and rowed ashore – and the lady did not go out again.

General utility boats

The types of boats used round here may be divided into two classes – the yawl and the square-stern. The yawls are a distinctly local type, that has developed according to the requirements of the locality.

---

[44] Also known as Creekland, a fine sandy bay

1895, Rackwick noust full of eight South Isles yoles ready to launch into the Pentland Firth for cod. No winch afforded here. The large round boulders had to be cleared away every spring.

Lightly built of a shallow draught, they are suitable for hauling on flat beaches, low-wooded to make them row easily, beam for carrying goods of all kinds, good rake fore and aft to manoeuvre easily when working the lobster creels, sharp clean ends for sailing – all these combined have evolved a type of boat for general utility which cannot be beaten anywhere.

First, I remember they were mostly under 15 feet of keel, but later Mr. Baikie built a great many of 14 feet 4 inches keel. These boats were at their peak about the time Mr. Ackroyd's regattas were held in Stromness in the last years of last century. We still have some of these fine boats, but the three sails have disappeared, except at Longhope regatta, where there is a special class for that type, but I am afraid that in spite of valuable cups and prizes, when the Viking crews that man these yawls disappear, the picturesque boats will disappear also.

When I first came to Stromness, a small dinghy was all we could get in which to cross to Hoy, and it was none too big for the waters we had to cross. This class has been greatly improved, and now we have as fine a lot of dinghies in Stromness as you will see anywhere.

Regatta of 50 years ago

I will finish by telling you about the first real regatta in which I sailed. It was all-comers race about 50 years ago. I was asked to be one of the crew of McDonald's wee Fifie. This was too tempting a chance to miss, and I was appointed to work the main sheet. The boat had jib, large dipping lug and dandy. A sail as far as Graemsay the night before the regatta, and our youthful crew felt ready for anything.

The start was by handicap and, as ours was the largest boat, we were last to get away. The wind was light westerly, the course the same as the big boats' course today. All went very well till we got to the buoy at the Skerries, where we had caught the leading boat. "About ship" shouted the skipper, and round she came. Down sail to shift it to the other side of the mast. The sail came down all right, but our bowman had not enough training, for the sail had not been hooked properly or something, and the traveller went to the top of the mast with no sail on it. I will not tell you any more, but we did not win that race. We consoled ourselves by saying that a dipping lug was not a suitable sail for racing.

Light South Isles yoles in Rackwick are very exposed on an open shore. The crew of six hauled boats up to the noust every day. Huge boulders were cleared by hand every Spring. c1920.

[This section continues with some brief reminiscences from Maurice Davidson's uncle Frank, now deceased, who lived and worked on Graemsay. It was clearly a hard life. Frank Davidson was born in Gorn, Graemsay, in 1915 and worked the croft, or farm as Orkney called its crofts, owned by the Laird of Graemsay and Orphir. When he tried to replace the old stone house built by his father, for his new family, the Laird casually told him how hard working he was, but he would have to increase his rent as this was a much better house! He demolished the new house rather than pay the increased rent, and years after moved to Aberdeen in 1960 where he could buy a farm. The Davidsons had farmed Gorn since at least the 1850s and Frank always looked back on his youth there with affection. It shows in his well-recollected memories, even at 100 years old. Frank died in 2017.]

A GRAEMSAY CROFTER

Some of Frank Davidson's memories from 1917 onwards, of Orkney yoles

"Graemsay, being an island without a pier in those days, made transport difficult, especially regarding cattle. They had to be loaded into a small boat one or two at a time, and rowed out to the mail boat where they were slung aboard with a derrick. This could only be done at a time convenient to the mail boat owners, which made it impractical to send our cattle to the mart on the mainland. We therefore had to rely on the tender mercies of the dealers.

Almost every crofter had one or two boats, mostly sailing yoles. There was no shelter on our side of the island, so they had to be hauled as soon as we landed. A boat was necessary for the transport of goods such as grain to the mill and meal from it, also coal, feed, fertiliser, eggs and groceries. As a rule, two or three crofters worked together; this facilitated the launching and hauling of the boat.

Fishing formed a fairly substantial part of our economy, but although white fish, such as cod and haddock, were at times fairly plentiful, the unpredictability of the weather made it impossible for us to guarantee a continuous supply. Therefore, we had no market; so we caught only what we could use ourselves. Some were salted for winter use.

Lobsters were the cash crop; this was usually managed from a dinghy with two of a crew, often two brothers, or father and son. It was possible to make up to £20 or more in a good season. This may not seem much now, but to a crofter it was probably twice his rent.

To those of us without the will power to adjust our sleeping pattern to suit both the ever-changing tide, which governed our fishing and our work on land, the going was rough, especially at harvest time and hay making and turnip hoeing ('singling' we called it in Graemsay)."

Harry Skinner and daughters launch their yole May every time, at the exposed Inner Noust, Graemsay, 1954. Wood linns help smooth the stony shore. Stern heightened for engine weight.

[Sheena Taylor rounds off this section by introducing us to a couple of yoles dating from 1890s (Sumato and the Hope) which are still in use today and describing the sorts of uses to which yoles of that vintage would have been put and how they were kept. She then takes us through the two World Wars with details provided mostly by her grandfather and father and shares her own memories of some other South Isles yoles which sadly are no longer with us. We learn more about the Sumato and its restoration in Section 6 while the Hope features in the final two articles of Section 7, with a dramatic recounting of sailing in dangerously stormy conditions in the Pentland Firth.]

ORKNEY YOLES IN HARNESS by Sheena Taylor

The two oldest seaworthy yoles we know of in Orkney are the *Jeanette*, built some time before 1893, later renamed *Sumato*, and *Hope*, based in South Ronaldsay, of roughly the same vintage.

It was only a few years earlier in 1888, when the main deliberations of the Napier Commission on crofting were completed, that a representative of the Commission visited Orkney to hear the individual submissions of 433 tenant farmers for relief of rent and rent arrears. That is recent enough for me to have heard from my grandfather, Arthur Burnett, about the benefits his forefathers, fairly cash-strapped tenants at Maraquoy on the outskirts of Stromness, had received following the Commission's rulings. The record of proceedings is held by the Stromness Library.

For many crofters at that time, either owning, or sharing ownership, of a yole provided an additional means of obtaining food mostly by long-line and creel fishing, as well as providing transport and access to essential commodities.

The boats were sheltered in natural or man-made 'nousts' above high water mark, sometimes launched down wooden tracks, called 'linns'. Two or three crews would assist each other in launching and recovery, either by manhandling the boats, or with the assistance of metal capstans or vertical wheels, some of which remain in situ along the coastline.

The remnants of stone-built fishing huts for storing both boats and fishing gear, and for providing shelter for fishermen on trips over a number of days, can also be found around the shore. Some, like those in the north coast of Birsay, have been renovated. Some communities also built stone shelters where they could change from their ordinary travelling clothes into 'better' outfits - their Sunday best, perhaps.

As well as fishing, yoles carried all kinds of cargo, including livestock.

Place names like Saltness, in Longhope's North Bay, indicate where that very necessary commodity for preserving food, mainly fish and meat, was landed. Excursions were also undertaken to bring salt to Rackwick from Stromness by sea, although grain was taken by foot from that settlement, using a route up the cliffs known as the Craig Gate, and onwards over the hills to the south of the island for milling, and the flour returned by the same method.

Passengers were carried by yole to markets, at one time 'feeing merkits', for hiring, and being hired as, farm workers.

Barswick noust, South Ronaldsay. The main landing for Swona yoles is nearby and fairly sheltered by cliffs. The stone hut was their changing room and toilet. Dinghy left in the noust.

The Lammas Market, which took place in August, was a particularly popular holiday, associated with what was sometimes called the 'first hairst' (first harvest).

Yole transport also took people to church services, weddings, funerals and social gatherings, like harvest-home festivals, as well as simply to shop and catch up on local and more general news.

In August 1914, young men in Orkney and elsewhere across the country, including teenagers too young to do so, who falsified their ages, rushed to enlist in what started as a European War, before it would be 'all over by Christmas'.

Unexpected work for local boats carrying material and passengers around the Flow came in 1915 with the construction near the farm at Ly Ness on Hoy, of the British Royal Navy Base, although Naval vessels were used later as the Base became established.

When cemeteries around the battlefields had been filled and memorials were planned, 1918/19 brought the 'Spanish' flu epidemic, which added further misery to five years of destruction by claiming the lives of many, especially young adults.

21st June 1919 also brought the scuttling of the interned German Fleet. The 'rescue' of coal, which would only get damp and go to waste, seemed sensible to several yole owners, it's said. A flurry of work came the way of some yole owners, as the salvage of the vessels began, but, as the venture gathered momentum, salvage companies used their own craft, sometimes manned by local boatmen. Recreational diving on the remaining wrecks has continued to provide work and income up to the present day.

The 1920s were years of change and some prosperity in the islands, as elsewhere. Peace had been restored after 'the war to end all wars'. Fishing was good, with often more than one lobster caught in creels: an abundance which was harvested without much thought for the morrow, resulting in much-depleted stocks, which have since recovered to a certain extent.

The early 1930s saw enthusiastic competition in regattas at which registered fishing yoles competed. As a youngster in Longhope, my father, Douglas Robertson, crewed with his kinsmen in the Johnston family boat, *Alert*, in competition with several larger yoles. He admired the magnificent *Gazelle* and the *Boray Man*, which may have had a long voyage, since the Holm of Boray lies to the south of Gairsay.

Then in 1939 all lights, including the carefully provided navigation lights round the coast, were extinguished. The order from Naval Command for them to be lit, when a convoy was expected, came by telephone to the Northern Light Board station in Stromness. It was not unusual for violin pupils receiving lessons there, to witness those phone calls. So much for security!

The devastating sinking by torpedo of *HMS Royal Oak*, with few survivors, when a submarine entered The Flow between the block ships in Kirk Sound, prompted the fast-flowing tidal channels to the east to be completely closed. No water flowed over the barriers after 1943, although it was a couple of years later before a roadway was added to provide a causeway for civilian traffic.

Moray Firth yole Robin, gunter rigged with jib and inboard motor. Built as a commercial fishing boat on the East Coast, with a large dipping lugsail. Motoring off North Ness, Longhope.

While providing easier communication with the mainland for the islands to the east, the causeways removed sea routes and altered tidal patterns on both sides of the barriers.

As merchant seamen and fishermen, bringing food to the nation, were constantly in danger of enemy attack, the fishing yole continued to be a great asset for local people.

After the War, depleted fish stocks meant boats had to go further afield, which they did in bigger engine-driven wooden vessels.

The introduction of smaller, faster, wooden pleasure craft, like the Merlin and Merlin Rocket, the Albacore and the Snipe, altered the attendance at regattas. Nevertheless, the regatta weeks of the middle decades of the last century continued to attract yoles, as before.

I had the privilege to be on the water (in a Snipe) at a Holm Regatta to which Jim Rosie in *Hood* had towed his smaller fishing dinghy, *Falcon*, all the way from his home in Stroma to compete with Walter Dunnet's elegant yole, *Laverne*, with Willie Groat's, *Saga*, and other vessels no longer on the water.

The motorised yole, *Rosebud*, belonged to the then Scapa Pier Harbour Master, John Wylie. In return for help in refurbishing *Rosebud* and adding a wheelhouse, John gave space in a shed by the shore between the Loch of Ayre and Holm Bay to my father, who was converting the *Otter* from a launch into a cabin cruiser. *Rosebud* became the property of Alfred Flett, Builder, in Holm, and passed onward to the Holm Sailing Club, as one of the club's safety boats, which has recently been refurbished once again by club members.

Several developments in transport and employment opportunities hastened the decline in yole use. The travel and freight-carrying function of yoles was taken over by ferries to both north and south isles, initially using the 'hoist and clunk' method, later replaced by roll-on roll-off facilities.

The establishment of the oil terminal, which took over much of the island of Flotta in the mid-1970s, brought welcome employment, as did the introduction of salmon cages, which were tended by specialised vessels. More recently, innovative, experimental tide and wave energy generating equipment also required more powerful, faster vessels than yoles.

One or two of the hundreds of yoles around the islands were cherished and sailed, or were skilfully restored, with the 'lines' of those beyond repair 'lifted' as the template for new vessels, a process also described in this book.

Other redundant yoles lay abandoned, untended in, or near, their nousts, with grass and nettles growing through the punctures made in the hulls by the hooves of kye (cattle): or perhaps lay outside a shed covered by a tarpaulin, 'in case they might be needed again' until the protective covering disintegrated. Perhaps the boats rested on rollers sheltered in a stone 'oot-bigging', where the hull 'gizened' – dried out and shrank - rendering the 'straiks' shrivelled and brittle.

Recent efforts of local boat builders and restorers have meant that the yole has been preserved. Sailors today can continue to enjoy glorious sea scenery and relish the good fortune of living and working in such wonderful surroundings, just as earlier sailors have done.

2011, Tall Ships Race in Stromness with a harbour full of sails.

Ron Bulmer's three sailed yole Grebe, at Hoy pier, newly launched in 2018 after much restoration. Built in 1973 in Burray, now based in Hoy, Grebe is 16 feet long and has an inboard engine.

Small South Isles spreet (sprit) sailed yole loaded with cod just caught off Flotta. The sails have been temporarily furled, easily done with this rig.

South Isles yole Emma, built 1912, Flotta, with original spreet (sprit) sail rig. Ian MacFadyen, skipper, reaching at full boat speed after the 2007 Longhope Regatta was stopped in F5-6 winds.

2017 Longhope Regatta showing some of the yoles resting at the sheltered pier. The sail down from Stromness through Scapa Flow's small isles is a great start to this most social event.

A very happy Billie Budge taking home two cups for his winning role on Gremsa's foresail, singing all the race round Longhope Bay. Commodore son Angus behind, 2018. Billie died in 2021.

Section 4 Learning to sail

[Sadly, the Orcadian dialect is on the decline. Yet, as Maurice Davidson's article below shows, it has a rich and diverse vocabulary. Gaelic never held sway in the Northern Isles, but Orcadian has drawn many words from the Scandinavian languages. It goes without saying that Yoles and the Orkney dialect are completely intertwined. Maurice introduces us in his own Orcadian voice to how he learned to sail as a teenager.]

YOLE SPIK by Maurice Davidson

"Ye've niver heard a yole spik[45]? Jist pit yer lug tae[46] the inside strakes at the stem head an' listen". The chatter of your bow wave breaking along the curved planks is music on the sea. I was 15 and hooked.

My dad was away a lot, skippering ships on the seven seas, but he had kept the *Seagull*, a peedie[47] 14-foot motor yole with lug sail, to fish off Hoy. He told me that Uncle Ji and him were handlining off the Kame[48] one day, haddock were thick when suddenly they stopped taking. Had they drifted off? Dad looked round and went white! He suddenly started the engine and motored back to Stromness as fast as he could. Ji complained it wis herd to pull his line in, whit wis the hurry? Dad pointed ahint[49] them - five big black fins, killer whales. They easily overtook the yole and swam round and round them. Dad swore the biggest stood straight up and spied at them! Then one orca, larger than the yole, swam under the boat upside down, white belly a few metres below. Dad felt sweat running down his face and hands in shock. One slight nudge and it was all over. He headed into the shallow sands, at the Pow on Hoy's shoreline, to move the whale below. As the orcas all surfaced in the shallows, dad reckoned he could smell haddock on their bad breath when they circled a few metres away. Bored, they aal left as suddenly as they appeared, with no aggressive motions – just curious? Certainly intelligent. Haddock are still thick around the Kame this year, and also orca, so these meetings can still happen.

Noo, I mind on that Doc Johnstone had the only sailing boat in Stromness, the toon still being in shock at the drowning of two dinghy sailors near the main pier in 1948.

My elder brother Dennis and his friend Willie had learnt to sail in the *Susie*, a solid clinker Orkney dinghy, and both had left for Sooth[50] at last. Now I could start sailing. Who wants to sail with an older teenage brother?

---

[45] You've never heard a yole speak
[46] Just put your ear to
[47] small
[48] A large headland on the northern tip of the island of Hoy
[49] behind
[50] South. "Gaan sooth" can range anywhere from Thurso to London and beyond.

Rosie's of Swona's huge 7.8M elliptic sterned Hood, their last boat built on Swona. Photo 1986 with the Davidson family.

Raja Brooke and I got the OK from a generous Doc, and set off in the *Susie* to the skirl of Shopping Week pipes, as the queen was crowned. A piece 'o piss, this sailing. We had seen how it was done. The flattie was rowed out to the moorings, crowded in sails and spars (canvas sails had to be dried in Doc Cromarty's washhouse) and us clad in rubber boots and oiled canvas jackets, bulky cork lifejackets were only for lifeboat crews. A few fishermen, bored with the radiant queen's speech, turned round to see this new harbour entertainment.

We eventually worked out where the two sails went, and the gret[51] heavy wooden rudder nearly took us over the stern as we hooked it on. "OK Raja, let go the moorings!" Well, we pulled the sails tight, pushed the boom this way and that, and still the south east wind jist[52] pushed us back onto the shore! By this time all the piers were lined by a jeering mob (all twelve) as the Shopping Queen and her retinue had departed. Gulls circled roond for wer[53] scraps.

Among cracking, flapping sails hitting my face, I jumped oot to push her off. "Beuy! She's heavy". Then oot 'o the sea a hero appeared rowing his dinghy, he tied on to wer bow and we aal rowed off the stones, back to wer mooring. A very patient Johnnie Simpson, the toon blacksmith, quietly explained how to use the sails and rudder. And off we sailed. We even tacked a slow stagger round to cheers from the now 30 faces above us. We opened Shopping Week that 1967, and it opened up a new life for Raja and me.

Efter wer success at the piers we swooped endlessly up and doon the harbour lik some white solan goose[54] fishing, the heavy wood boom knocking sail sense into our heads every gybe. But then a whole string of eight big Buckie seine netters steamed in to toast wer lovely Shopping Week queen. How do we sail through this lot back to wer mooring? Heart banging and throat dry, we crossed right behind one of these snorting monsters, to more "foreign" East coast Doric banter this time.

Raja lay on the foredeck and hooked the mooring buoy, but not for long! The art of slowing up into the wind was new, and Raja flew off into the harbour firmly holding the buoy. I grabbed the flattie as it passed and tied off, with difficulty. More cheers from the piers! Getting Raja to let go of the buoy was harder, as he couldn't swim. But he wis a queek learner!

By the next Longhope regatta we were seasoned sailors. Early that morneen[55] Doc loaded aal the supplies for the day, mainly crates of his fearsome brew, plus Archie, Mac …and me! Promotion at last, Jimi Neep the butcher had let me off my bike delivery job that Saturday, but only because the Doc asked him. Raja worked for a much sterner shopkeeper so couldn't come.

In the pink sunrise we drift oot o' the herber[56] – three green bottles of brew relieving the tension. No wind and the ebb tide flowing.

---

[51] large
[52] just
[53] our
[54] gannet
[55] morning
[56] harbour

2010 Longhope Regatta with ten yoles, the most ever seen together in recent years - R to L, Lotte, Mohican, Gremsa, Robin, Lily, Helga, Lizzie 2, Family Pride, Emma and Eve.

Ginger motors round Ness in his white Thames police launch, his Hoy ferry, jeers at us in his Cockney lilt, then throws us a rope and off we tow across the tide. The cost of the hire - two green bottles.

We attempt to sail along Graemsay. And Alfie takes pity on us in the *Evelyn*, his huge seine netter, racing off to Scrabster with the night's haddock from Skaill Bay. I grab his thick, worn hawser and literally bend it round wer mast, it would fit nothing else! And off we surged at eight knots, a mountainous wave splitting either side of the bow, coming over the deck when we hit the Bring tide. We aal shat wersels[57], the *Susie*, ropes and us aal shakan lik[58] mad. Sittan doon, wer stern wave wis so big we couldn't see the lighthouse. Alfie nonchalantly throttles doon to speak to some Americans diving on the Fleet, with their owld German pinnace aal glinting wey bress[59]. What fleet I ask? I was unaware of aal the German ships hivan a[60] rust below. The Doc ups and looses Alfie's huge towrope as fast as he can. Another three green bottles are passed over to Alfie's happy crew.

How we enjoyed the relief of a quiet sail ower to Fara, the bacon rolls and banter, and fresh coffee. Whit's fresh coffee? BANG!!! The buddom[61] boards ripped out below wer feet as I fell on them. Campbell's salvage divers had blown their charges on the German cruiser *Karlsruhe*, 25 metres below! Laughing and collecting stunned cod floating up nearby, we were handed one a piece, as an American peace gesture! They couldn't be fresher.

The Longhope regatta was an endless hot day of drifts, through their specially laid long seaweed and surprisingly fast start tides, which are still a tradition today. I helmed the whole day as the crew gave up, thanks to bad wind and good brew! This was the Doc's ONLY day off each year when he could relax, and everyone acknowledged it.

You kent[62] the race course by the trail of red and green cans from aal the three sailed yoles, hid wis their ONLY day off too and everyone was in good form. We came last in both races and received more red Labour cans than anyone, as they sailed past.

Up to the Royal – to what wis Whadiam's bar – for beer and the fishermen's crack and banter too! Seemingly, the local yole crews throw their red Export cans to port and green Pale Ale McEwans to starboard, jist in case a sudden fog comes doon ower us, so we aal can find wer way back tae the bar.

As still is normal, everyone claimed aal the many yole collisions during the regatta wer always on starboard. The stories jist got bigger, and I believed them aal. Little did we ken then that these fishy tales from the freendly lifeboat crew were aal at their last regatta.

---

[57] ourselves
[58] shaking like
[59] with brass
[60] heaving with
[61] bottom
[62] knew

South Isles yole Mohican owned and sailed by Commodore Angus Budge at the Longhope Regatta 2019.

The *Susie* was awarded a large silver cup, for the first, and only (!) local dinghy, as she was built in Lyness. And the Doc got the biggest applause of the day, a real community award.

We aal admired the Rosies' huge elliptical sterned yole at the pier, especially as the skipper kindly offered us a tow. And off we went to Lyness towed next to their elegant dinghy, the *Falcon* (built on Swona where they lived, not local), before they headed off to the Pentland Firth, that being their ONLY day off for the year also.

We staggered onto our mooring back in Stromness in the grimleens[63], and jist as weel that there were no jeering crowds there. What a chance to experience sailing and life. I never looked back. Thanks for everything, Doc.

In 1970, the Sea School under an enthusiastic Captain Robbie Sutherland's leadership, offered to teach youngsters how to sail a yole. I'd niver sailed a yole before and was soon hooked on their easy curves and simple spreet[64] sail rig. They smoothly rode over the seas and didn't flip ower in a squall.

Sir Alec Rose, that famous and unassuming round-the-world yachtsman, came up for a holiday at the Stromness regatta in 1970. A very humble man, he related understated tales of Cape Horn and the Southern Ocean. He presented his book to all the winners after the sailing, even the slower three-sailed yoles! I sailed the *Family Pride*, Dan Kirkpatrick's old yole, against Davie Davidson in the *Elsie*, the Johnston boys' yole. Alec had niver seen yoles or sprit sails and thought we had something here that the Sooth Coast had lost out to sleek, modern yachts. He came oot fur a sail the next day, blazer, kep[65] and aal, before flying off.

Friday afternoons at school were for sailing. Under Robbie, we took thirty kids oot in the three yoles, a dinghy and a huge whaler – with a loud Commander Clouston at the helm. And dare you to cross his bow!

One Friday, I sailed the *Family Pride* across to Graemsay, and on the way back had to cross the old *Hoy Head*'s wash – and promptly burst the port bow open! Eight old iron nails had rusted through on fower[66] strakes. Sea flushed through the gap on every wave, soaking aal the five bairns[67] we had onboard, to their delight but not to the delight of Raja and me. We tacked to keep the port bow oot o' the water, shakan as we expected more rusty rivets to burst at any time.

We niver sailed the *Family Pride* again. The *Elsie* seemed more solid but slow; and as no one else wanted to sail her, she became wer favourite. I sailed Sooth Isles yoles *Elsie* and *Pansy* aal summer and every summer until I qualified as an architect in 1975. The *Family Pride* was eventually totally renewed by Kevin Kirkpatrick, with a great job from "John A" Mowat in Brims. The *Tiger*, a large 6.3-metre Sooth Isles yole, was also left to rot in Coplands' Dock, along with the *Family Pride*, but no family came to her rescue, only the chainsaw and cremation.

---

[63] evening light
[64] sprit
[65] cap

[66] four
[67] children

The Family Pride hauled out in the sheltered bay in front of the Longhope Lifeboat station.
She is a typical South Isles yole with fairly full bilges to lift to the tidal seas here.

I headed Sooth, then East, to live and work in Borneo, and only sailed alternate summers, to see the owld widen yoles slowly gizen up[68], fall to pieces and disappear into a blue lowe[69]. I needed a yole to enjoy sailing in our six weeks in Orkney, and Deb and our kids were keen on fishing. At Sylvia Wishart's Simmer Dim[70] party in 1996, I plied my brother with brew, but he still wasn't keen on having a new yole, built by Ian. My cousin was next to us, and turned roond to offer to build a yole if I would pay for the wid. Hans wir shook on the spot, and launched with another glass of Sylvia's malted nectar. And three years later, the *Gremsa* was built by my cousin.

In the late 1960s, my "uncle" James o' Garson came ower fae Graemsay, to retire to a pier hoose in Stromness. His dad and he built their 18-foot motor yole *Jane* in owld Merrag o' Hourabreck's cottage, and had to take the gable oot, to get her oot. He wis keen on creeling for lapsters[71] and we started setting 38 single creels, home-made in the winter, widen with stone bases and knitted nets on iron bows. We were the last old-style yole, laying creels all roond Hoy Soond and Graemsay, with every creel hauled by me to keep fit! This continued while at university and helped pay for my five years' studies. It was a huge learning curve for me. James had lived aal his life roond Graemsay and knew every rock, tide and fish in detail, a generous man wi' terrific local knowledge.

James wid always luk at the sky, sunrise and sunset, and forecast the weather without the sun's influence. He wid also check seaweed motion in the open sea near the beacon, a harbinger of weather oot west. And check the birds. Small things have big results.

We hunted every type of fish just to taste them. Night fishing! Tied to the *Inverlane*[72] shipwreck – which finally sank a few years ago, rearing up out of fierce Burra Soond tides, wer boat lit by two old oil lamps to attract aal the big black congers living in the wreck. We caught plenty!

Often fower or seex feet of writhing, spinning muscle weighing up to 28 lbs, with huge snapping mouths lined in needle sharp teeth! An' Scrabster paid weel for them. Efter a herd tug o' war on the handline, they went wild on wer floorboards. But throw a weet owld cloot[73] on them and instant peace descends. In the flickering lamplight, sometimes one would slither off in the dark. And one bit James's wader boot, missed his toe; but James couldn't get the teeth oot, an' he hobbled aboot in his sock for a cowld couple o' hours.

Another night in Burra Soond saw a very excited Eric heave in a small conger over his head! Unfortunately, it smashed the bow lamp overboard and lit oil spilled all over the prow, and into the sea round the bow. With the petrol tank nearby, this got exciting! Buckets of sea water were thrown with abandon in the darkness. And aal the congers laughed at us. Night fishing was niver dull!

---

[68] dry up
[69] flame
[70] around midnight in Orkney when the sun barely sets in midsummer
[71] lobsters

[72] The bow of the *Inverlane* was used as a blockship protecting the entrance into Scapa Flow, between Hoy and Graemsay. It was a feature for many years long after hostilities ceased, until an Atlantic storm finally drove the bow to the seabed.
[73] wet old cloth

Debbie, Bill and Maurice fish off the Kame of Hoy on South Isles yole Gremsa, sailing there on the ebb tide and sailing back to Stromness with the strong flood tide, but little wind. 2015.

Off to haul creels round the Klestran[74] Skerries one day, we had Eric and Len onboard for a day trip to Graemsay efter the work wis done. From a normal day with a fair breeze, I noticed an unusual line of dark cloud behind Hoy. Later the wind suddenly fell, and James whispered that we'd better get oot o' here, pointing to the white line of sea oot West. I stopped hauling and he handed me the helm, as he couldn't see through his glasses when there was any spray. And soon there was plenty of spray. I turned the yole towards Stromness, but the huge pan loaf cloud, a line squall, was on us in minutes and the wind rose to gale force with a bang.

White spray blinded wer eyes and the chaos of crashing waves scared the lif' oot o' me. We were trapped in shallow, tidal waters on a lee shore - not a great place to be. Waves started to come ower the bow, however slow I set the throttle, as seas were now breaking freely. "The shore!" James shouted in the gale. Surely he didna mean to beach the boat? My eyes went white in shock. I shoved the helm hard over and throttled up to get quickly round to a quieter area, and there weren't many. We took a sea or two over the stern, and James moved forward. Me mooth went dry as we raced towards Klestran's sandy beach in cascading waves. I braced for the landing. "Herd ower tae starboard! NOW!" and we proved yoles can lift across sharp, breaking seas as we shot into the shelter behind a rocky arm of the skerries, in just six feet of sea.

We spent a happy hour anchored there, throwing aal wer baitfish to enthusiastic selkies[75] cavorting on the surf. Local knowledge is everything in these high-energy isles.

The line squall passed and we headed home, in silence the whole way. A close call. We spoke to the lifeboat secretary that day, and he said he was about to call out the lifeboat for us, but couldn't see where we were in all the spray and white water. We had disappeared behind the skerry.

My mother wondered why we were back so early.

---

[74] Clestrain

[75] seals

South Isles motor yole Jane built by crofters James o' Garson and his father in Graemsay between the wars. Flitting furniture across to the Lighthouse pier, Graemsay.

South Isles yole Gremsa with Willie and Maurice on their 2006 North Isles sail, landing here at Gairsay, by their old Viking J-style stone pier. The rebuilt Langskaill of Sweyn Asleifarson is behind.

[Willie Tulloch was born and brought up in Stromness. As a youngster he was always keen on the sea, spending his summer holidays on the water, either in his flattie or out with the local fishermen at the creels. After finishing schooling, he embarked on a sea career, starting off on deck and progressing to Master. Now retired, he continues to sail regularly in his yacht Ragna.]

THE SEA AND HOW I GOT INTO SAILING by Captain Willie Tulloch

I was brought up in Stromness in a house adjacent to the sea and was always down near the water. When the tide was out, I was in the ebb and when the tide was in, I was on the water.

My first experience of having something that floated and could carry a person was with my tractor tube. With a net tied across its bottom and a small batten across the top as a seat and a home-made paddle, that was me ready to go out in my first craft. Great. I had much fun with it until, one day, a westerly wind blowing across the harbour and catching my craft blew me across to the Holms, the small islands on the east of the harbour. The tractor tube disappeared soon after, and I assumed that that was down to my father, but nothing much was said by my parents and shortly after I became the proud owner of a small flattie (the local flat-bottomed rowing boat). The year was 1962.

I had that flattie for a few years until I heard Bunt Knight was selling his one for the sum of £10. I acquired this one and, it being bigger and more stable than the former one, I was able to add a mast, which was an old cloth pole cut to size and fitted by old Pia Anderson, and an old sheet cut up carefully by my dear mother for a sail. So equipped, away I went for my first experience of sailing, rowing to the south end of the harbour and sailing back with a southerly.

It was drilled into me, that there should be no going outside the harbour.

A few years later, on a Boys Brigade trip to Fair Isle, Dennis Davidson and myself, both very keen on boats, spent as much time as possible down at the nousts[76] looking at the Fair Isle skiffs.

I thought, backed up by Dennis, that a suitable skiff was there which I could buy. So, I promptly contacted my father for a loan and received a reply: NO WAY.

But all was not lost. Dennis and I discussed the matter with Dr Johnston, a local GP who was very interested in teaching the younger generation the art of sailing. He told us that he thought the skiff was unsuitable for us, but then kindly offered Dennis and me the use of his own boat, and thrown into the deal, he taught us to sail.

---

[76] A boat haul, a shallow depression where Orkney yoles were overwintered

Willie Black's large gunter rigged South Isles yole Valkyrie hauled up Alfie Young's slip for cleaning before the Stromness Regatta, 1969.

In return we also had to paint and maintain his boat, the *Susie*, an Orkney-style dinghy built by Davie Wilson in Lyness, which we did until Dennis went to university to study to be a naval architect and I went off to make the sea my career.

In 1974, I was looking to buy a yole, having been interested for some time to acquire one, but none were available.

Whilst working on my first job at sea on the *Watchful*[77], I heard that Sammy Doull from Longhope was thinking of selling his yole named the *Emma*. I contacted him and found that he would take £30 for her, no more and no less. In those days I did not have that amount of spare cash and so contacted my sailing friend Jock Davidson, who was happy to go half shares in her.

After the deal was clinched and *Emma* put in the water for us to sail away, Sammy came down to the boat with a name plate and a galvanised bucket. "Never change the name of her, always keep the nameplate on the stern, and you will need the bucket to bail out on the passage back to Stromness", he said. She had not been in the water for a couple of years and was dried out through standing under cover, so was going to leak for the first few sails.

Jock and I felt like lords and were so proud of ourselves sailing her into Stromness. We had *Emma* for many years of great fun. Jock then got married and I bought out his share. In 1977, I bought new sails for her at the staggering cost of £150.

In 1994 my son Scott and I had been fishing out west in the *Emma* and that night the fog came in very quickly. I had to make a quick decision as to whether to take the long way in and possibly get caught in the fog or, instead, to cut across the ebb tide, which I decided to do. Just after we were clear of the tide rip Scott said "Look at the water level - I think we should start pumping". We were taking in so much water that, as we were rounding the beacon, I thought about beaching her there, but in the end, we managed to get her into the Navigation School pier in the harbour.

I had Ian Richardson, the local boat-builder, down to the boat the next day and we found the garboard strake on the starboard side had opened up.

Ian's words to me were: "I do not know where I will finish up cost-wise if I start to fix her. She is an old boat. Have you ever thought about having a new one built?"

Ian duly started building a 17.5-foot larch on oak yole for myself later that year. I had her launched in June 1995 and named her *Helga* after my daughter. *Helga* has proved to be an excellent craft and a pleasure to sail.

On my retirement in 2005, when speaking to my son Scott about boats, he said to me: "This is the time for you to have what you have always wanted."

---

[77] A summer ferry running between Stromness, Hoy, Lyness and Flotta run by Bremner & Co

Scott, Helga and Willie Tulloch sailing their gunter yole Helga, built by Ian Richardson, Stromness 1995, based on the Emma, Flotta. NLV Pole Star tied up at her pier in Stromness, 2001.

I took his advice and acquired the *Ragna*, a 36-foot Rival yacht, with cutter rig. I could not have a finer yacht. She has good sea-keeping qualities, is a pleasure to sail and has excellent manoeuvring ability. I duly passed *Helga* on to my brother who sailed her for many years before in turn passing her on. She is still sailed regularly in Stromness.

In 2010, I came across a Norwegian faering (4-oared boat) in Stromness. This was a traditional Norwegian clinker-built boat, designed to be sailed and rowed by two people, with four oars. She had been built in the Hardangerfjord in Norway by a Fair Isle builder as his apprenticeship project, and eventually made her way to Stromness. I immediately fell in love with her and bought her. I named her Thor, in honour of my mother who was called Thora. I have sailed her out to the Old Man of Hoy and also taken her down to the Portsoy traditional boat festival. She is a lovely craft that I am keeping for my grandbairns to sail in.

As for now, I am hoping for many more years of excellent sailing on my marvellous yacht *Ragna*.

Willie Tulloch in the traditional Orkney dinghy Dido, built by Baikie's, Stromness, over a hundred years ago. Gremsa behind, both moored to the beach in Graemsay.

OYA South Isles yole Lily with traditional three sail rig. Many folk have sailed her, and early on in 2008-10 she was helmed by young Steven Flett (17 - 19) and his younger crew.

South Isles yole Gremsa showing three sails and spreets (sprits) taking the Primary School children out for their first sail from Stromness Nav School. Bill and Thorfinn assist.

Flaws' pier in 1969 with Johnnie Flaws' small South Isles yole craned up on their pier for the winter, along with his flattie. The yole was moored with a large stone off the pier.

Mr Laird, the last crofter on Copinsay, transporting emergency hay for his kye (cattle) on the small isle, during the dry summer of 1942. Single mast dipping lugsail used.

21(!) three sailed South Isles yoles, all spreet (sprit) rigged, 18 feet long, sailing at the South Ronaldsay Regatta. The stone pier being built is where Banks' ferry operates now. c1880.

Section 5 Regattas

[Orkney novelist and historian Eric Linklater [1899 - 1974] was of Orcadian parentage, but was actually born in Wales. However, he saw war service in Orkney, and formed a deep bond with the place of his forebears. He sailed his large elliptical sterned yole, the Skua, in local seas. By way of accolade George Mackay Brown, the renowned Stromness author, considered this the best description of a regatta he had seen. The Skua is now in the custody and care of the Orkney Historic Boat Society. The editors cannot imagine the courage (or foolhardiness) needed to set a spinnaker when the wind strength necessitated reefing the mainsail well down as described.]

EXTRACT FROM "THE MAN ON MY BACK" by Eric Linklater

"Nowhere are gales more loud and furious, nowhere is the peace more deeply spread on lake and hill and the inland sea. I have sailed my boat out of Stromness, on a regatta day, with four turns of the mainsail round the boom and my heart convulsive as a dying cockerel in my throat. The boat to weather with its mast leaning over my weather side, and my lee deck smothered in a furious sea, the tiller pulling like a bull on a rope. To the harbour mouth in a black yell of the wind, and pointing to the squall – mainsheet in – across to the tide on Graemsay shore. Tide and wind in opposition, a maniac stream with the strength of the moon in its whirly flood, and so to the lighthouse and a new course to the Ireland shore. Open water, a grim beat to windward and the pump sucking dry though water was washing deeply in the lee belly of the boat. Then round again to meet the squalls that came screaming from the hill. Once I was slow in luffing and over she went till the sea covered the lee deck and like a weir came pouring in. This delayed us, and at the next buoy there was an angry scuffle with the boat that till then had been behind, but turning on the northward leg we set the spinnaker, steadied and pumped her dry, and then like a homing gannet, but hissing louder than a lair of dragons, raced the curling waves. A broad reach then, the tiller so heavy that my breath came sobbing with the pain of holding it, and into the tormented harbour. Then out again, another round, and now we were doubly drenched, with spray and sweat, and the squalls on the Ireland shore were fiercer than ever, the homeward run more swift and splendid. But before we crossed the line the gale was already whimsical, and though we passed the mark-buoy in a flurry that laid us nearly flat, a moment later, like a stare of surprise, there was a minute's calm and we stood upon a level keel.

The start of the evening race was as leisurely as old ladies playing croquet, and an hour later every boat was becalmed. They floated like feathers on a village pond, the islands lay at anchor to unmoving shadows, and the sky stood in a breathless trance. When the slow twilight came, the dreaming water met the light of stars without a quiver.

Eric Linklater's elliptic sterned Skua built in 1934 by Willie Ritch, Deerness for £46 often helmed by Jock Stout, Pole Star piermaster, NLB. Split cod are drying on the shore behind.

In such weather, in a boat that soared lazily and softly fell upon the sleeping pulse of the Atlantic, I have lain below the great cliffs of Hoy, that rise eleven hundred feet sheer above the sea. In the evening light they were red as a wine-stain, and flowing from their pillared walls, a tropic air, came the gathered warmth of the day.

Such a day I have spent on Scapa Flow, when the surface of the sea was like polished marble, in the distance reflecting light, but overside impenetrably black. Save the engine throb, there was no sound but the liquid fall of the bow-wave, a crystal semi lune that cut the stillness like a plough, and heaped upon it a sparkling ridge of rough translucent water. On the one side, below a nacreous sky, were the round hills of Hoy, and on the other a coloured shore that stained the reflecting sea with pale red, and yellow corn. Rounding a low point, the boat came into shallow water, a green transparency that showed a bottom of pale sand on which tall seaweed grew. A shoal of little fish fled from the shadow of the boat. A flock of kittiwakes, startled, rose from a stony beach and doubled their number in the mirror of the sea. The stiff and sudden clamour of their wings was clearly audible, and the down-draught of their flight struck the wet beach like a breeze from the hill. A mile away, in a ripe field, a reaper clattered softly through yellow straw. A cormorant, with reaching neck and sluggish wings, flew past us with jarring noise.

We crossed to the island of Hoy, and in a shallow bay anchored on a glittering shore. Here and there, in a submarine dust storm, a small flounder was put to flight, and presently in the floor of the sea we could discern, like tiny yellow jewels, the eyes of cockles buried in the sand. A seal, with mild inquisitive gaze, swam slowly round. Two or three miles away, on a shoal called the Barrel of Butter, lay a whole rookery of seals, somnolent in the afternoon, and like lean philosophers a few herons pondered the ebb. The southern isles stood on a ridge of light above the sea, and to the north-east, above the town of Kirkwall, rose the cathedral spire of St. Magnus."

Reproduced with permission from the estate of Eric Linklater.

Laverne on its last sail, Andy Dunnet at the helm. An old Baikie classic elliptical stern yole variant, built to win races, in their yard next to the OYA pier. Sold South.

1938, the last Stromness Regatta pre WW2, with large racing gunter rigs on yoles, dinghies, and elliptic sterned yoles Laverne and Skua in the centre even sporting home-made spinnakers.

[Orkney hosts a series of six regattas every Saturday from late June (except for 2020), when sailing classes of every sort, including yoles, compete for a variety of trophies. Such occasions are renowned for their social aspects, as much as for what happens on the water. The following article contains extracts from Sheena Taylor's reports for OYA members in 2017, that year being notable for the re-introduction of Burray's regatta. One of the regular helmsmen of the OYA's yole for many years was Allie Kirkpatrick, who managed to win many a regatta cup, and features below. For the yoles, the regattas also give the opportunity for lengthy sails between the four locations in the Flow, when tides and wind can make the journey quite challenging! On the return from Holm to Stromness, the Helga had just tied up safely in Stromness harbour, when the wind picked up. The Lily, half an hour behind from being sailed single-handed by Angus Budge, was just entering the harbour when a gust nearly capsized her, but good seamanship prevailed and all was well.]

2017 ORKNEY REGATTA REPORTS by Sheena Taylor

Longhope and Holm regattas

The run-up to **Longhope Regatta** on 2nd July saw three regular yole sailors heading off to Shetland; two more displaying yole *Waterwitch* as a two-master at Portsoy Boat Festival and others involved in various pursuits. A forecast threatening strong wind immediately following the event put participation of other visiting yoles in doubt.

As Commodore of Longhope Sailing Club, Angus Budge took it on himself to sail *Lily* from Stromness to Longhope, the boat to be skippered there by Steven Flett, in competition with *Gremsa* and Longhope local boats. Maurice Davidson and Thorfinn Johnston sailed *Gremsa* to Longhope, camping there for a few days.

We all enjoyed a great day on the water, excellent hospitality and banter.

Gremsa and *Lily* reappeared in Stromness during the next week, once the strong winds had abated. Did they think they could evade the harbour surveillance system by arriving at 23:20? Angus undertook to sail *Lily* to Holm on Friday evening before **Holm Regatta** on Saturday 8th July. He can have had little time for sleep before setting sail again at 06:00 in *Helga*.

Christine and Laura came up to Holm from Longhope in a R.I.B., with Christine joining me as crew in *Lily* with Angus as skipper, while Laura joined *Helga*. *Helga* 'ferly flung doon' the gauntlet giving us a good view of her stern the whole way round both races.

Immediately after racing, the crew not returning to Stromness were whisked ashore by safety boats, to allow *Helga* and *Lily* to make best speed back to Stromness, before the freshening south westerly could increase further as forecast. The Longhope ladies also headed homewards in their R.I.B. at a rate of knots.

Have you counted the number of roughly three-hour trips Angus made in the nine-day period? Five in all, which makes about 15 hours moving boats to add to the time spent racing. Worth a mention in dispatches, don't you think?

Holm hospitality and humour was as excellent as ever.

Dr. Cromarty's new yole Lotte built by Ian Richardson and racing in her home port at the Longhope Regatta 2017.

South Isles yole Pansy reaching at full speed after the Longhope Regatta, 2006 with Kevin Kirkpatrick at the helm. She needs some hull repairs now before going afloat, soon hopefully.

Stromness Regatta

The forecast for **Stromness Regatta** on Saturday 15th July promised light winds at first, rising later in the day with buckets of rain…and that's just what we got: about one inch of rain over the three hours.

The Stromness based yoles, *Gremsa, Helga, Lily, Solwen* and *Waterwitch*, with *Mohican* from Longhope, set off from the north end of the bay immediately following the Hamnavoe's departure. A tow from the rescue boat was gladly accepted by *Lily* after a slightly late leaving of the berth caused by the need to find extra waterproofs.

Shortly after the start, the downpour began. By the time the boats were underway to the first mark, there was enough wind for 'sittan oot.' As the race progressed, the mainsail formed an efficient catchment device, channelling water along the boom to run off the gooseneck in a steady stream aiming for the back of the neck.

A triangular course was set: Navershaw Bay, Bay of Ireland and Mallow Bank, with a beat and downwind sausage between the last two buoys. First time Stromness Regatta sailors had been told the Mallow Bank buoy would be found by heading from the buoy set in the Bay of Ireland towards Hoy High, but visibility was too poor to see the lighthouse! Safety boats at the buoys were a welcome sight, while wind and tide in the same direction made rounding that windward mark one of the race's challenges.

There was a coldish lull in the shelter of the harbour while all the boats completed the first race. Having shared what little refreshments we had aboard, the second race began (without *Gremsa*, who had retired as the crew were too wet to carry on) with a competitive start over a shorter, simple triangular course.

The wind had risen sufficiently to send spray aboard. "Aer thoo gettan weet?" I thought of dodging inboard to give the spray a chance of reaching those further back in the boat, but decided the conditions were a bit uppity for 'muckan aboot'.

A 'batt' of wind heeled over one of the yachts at a crazy angle …and, suddenly, nearby *Waterwitch's* sail was gone. The safety boat at the Bay of Ireland buoy was quick to assist.

Our skipper chose a course to take advantage of the changed tidal conditions, which meant we were no longer able to see the other boats in the worsening visibility. Allie's glasses were running with water anyway. Everyone's main concern on getting back to the marina was to get warm and dry as quickly as possible.

While we enjoyed the hospitality of the host club in the Golf Clubhouse, congratulations went to *Solwen* on a day of success in both races. Those wins earned both the now-separated Corrigal Cup and Blue Riband as well as a place in the written record of winners in the presentation box, the first two being Eric Linklater in *Skua* in the mid-1930s.

When consulted on who to ask to retrieve the capsized yole, the RNLI chose to tow *Waterwitch* in to prevent the submerged hull becoming a hazard to shipping in the approaches to the harbour. In calm water, she was easily righted, electrics and inboard engine to be restored: no-one hurt and Rod took the whole event in his stride - though, of course, he'd rather it hadn't happened.

One and a half inches of rain fell during the Stromness Regatta, 2017. South Isles yoles Waterwitch and Solwen singing in the rain with oars, before the start.

Burray Regatta

Burray Regatta, re-introduced after many years, was held on 22nd July in idyllic conditions. The only yole present was Angus Budge's, *Mohican*, which he'd brought from Longhope for the event. He and his crew no doubt enjoyed the sun, the brisk, steady sailing breeze from the east with a flat sea and only a gentle ebb in the enclosed bay created in the shelter of the 4th Barrier.

The local Lifeboat Guild had arranged a fund-raising day, providing teas and welcome food during the midday break between races. The Longhope lifeboat and crew arrived to support the event. Suitably clad in his smart red buoyancy aid, Hector, Angus' pedigree Scottie and crewman who'd travelled in *Mohican*, was clearly delighted to see his lifeboat and people, so he could keep them under surveillance, as is his wont.

Over lunch, a daft raft race provided additional diversion in the sunshine, bruises obtained in combat being proudly displayed by some participants.

The green on the waterfront near Duncan's former boat-building yard accommodated a fair-sized crowd of onlookers, everyone enjoying the nostalgic air of a genial village carnival with a tuneful traditional band playing under a canvas shelter.

Westray Regatta

Preparations for **Westray Regatta** on 29th July were all made in advance of the arrival of the special ferry carrying boats of all sizes from Kirkwall to Pierowall. The boats are hoisted to the pier, masts set, launched and rigged. In the case of yoles, some expert tractor and trailer reversing down the narrow slipway is needed.

Competitors arrive by various methods, sailing from Shetland and neighbouring islands, by ferry over a couple of days and some even by air to Papa Westray and short ferry to Pierowall. Some visiting sailors took spare crew places or sailed in club boats. There were 46 boats: yachts, yoles, skiffs, lugs, cats, Snipes, Lasers, a Wayfarer, a fancy new three-person RS Quest, and Bugs - sailed by juniors.

A steady north westerly breeze allowed a moderately long race in the morning. Wind dropped away to nothing over the lunch break, returning from almost 180° in time for the afternoon race start, enabling the same course to be used in the opposite direction. The shortened course procedures were used when the wind dropped again in the later afternoon. At several stages the sky darkened around us, but the torrential downpours in other areas of the islands and to the south of us in Westray stayed clear of Pierowall Bay.

As the Westray Lifeboat Guild, like the one in Burray, was also making the day a fund-raising event, the Kirkwall lifeboat visited during the afternoon. Once the racing is over, the travelling boats have to be de-rigged, put on trailers and re-loaded on the ferry, with the yole fraternity struggling not to keep the others waiting.

The prize-giving, sponsored by Scapa distillery, was well attended. Westray's legendary, truly remarkable evening meal followed, with a dance later in the evening. Those of us fortunate enough to be able to stay over the next day enjoyed the most glorious sunshine, wonderful scenery and warmth. Another really enjoyable event!

North Isles skiffs in close competition at the start line of the 2006 Westray Regatta. All these locally made boats have home-made timber Bermudan masts and standard dinghy sails.

Kirkwall Regatta

Kirkwall Regatta on 2nd August had a few surprises in store in what has proved to be the most challenging of the season's six regattas.

Lily, the only yole, raced against three visiting skiffs in the morning. Strong winds from the North West kicked up a bit of a sea, causing some early retirals and some capsizes of dinghies and cats. We would have liked to reef, but the boat was not set up for that. With time passing, the competitive spirit rose to the fore. With stop-watch at the ready we made a good start. It was busy work balancing the boat, and controlling the tugging jib on downwind legs. An extra person would have been useful.

Beating and reaching, I could - just - hold the jib sheet secured round a specially placed clip for that purpose, once it had been 'sweated' in by Angus. Retrieving that tension, if wind had to be spilled, was another two-person task. Backing the jib properly on the tack took extra concentration for, once the pressure on the windward sheet was eased, the sail flew out too far and too fast. On one tack, the same strong arm assisted, for we needed the jib's power not to 'miss stays' in those conditions. How useful pulleys, judiciously used jammers, maybe even a self-tailing winch, would be! I know: not traditional! But a ratchet fitment of some sort would be great.

As the yoles and skiffs sailed into the basin for a welcome lunch in the Girnel, we had a longer break than dinghy crews. We learnt that the Kirkwall Lifeboat was on its way to Stronsay to attend a fund-raising event. Skippers consulted their crews on whether they would sail in the afternoon. "I'll go if you go," said one. Allie asked Angus, "Will we go again?" Yes, he would. (No-one asked me.)

One of the skiffs, with an extra person on board, and *Lily* with the three of us, headed for the more sheltered course, reset within the bay. As we untied from our temporary berth alongside a small fishing boat, a sudden 'swaap' jerked the sail from Allie's hands and the claw on the boom neatly swiped his glasses off into the water without hitting him at all. He has spares, he says.

The impression from the shore, that there was less wind in the afternoon, was inaccurate; but there was considerably less sea to contend with. A lot of wind was spilled from both sails and the helming skipper's vigilance was crucial, particularly when running and gybing.

"Neat bit of sailing, Boys, including the backward sailing!" came from a sailor, who took our bow rope, as we returned to the same marina finger berth we'd left in the morning. I thought so too. No choice, since the outboard and fuel were on the pontoon and extracting the oars from under the thafts (thwarts) would have taken too much time, and used up the limited sea room within the marina.

The evening prize-giving in the Girnel was followed by a most enjoyable dance to music from the Stronsay Band.

For the first time this year a new cup was awarded to the first skipper and boat combination in each class calculated over all six regattas. For the yole class, that went to Allie Kirkpatrick, in spite of his only taking part in three regattas due to other sailing activities – a fitting testament to his consistent skill.

Just a little longer to enjoy the boats, before they are lifted for winter storage in advance of the equinoctial gales.

Two North Isles yoles well behind a Deerness built yole (Ivy) in an old Kirkwall Regatta c1935.
All yoles are rigged with the new high gunter sails in cotton to race well into the wind.

[The Westray regatta is renowned as the premier location for regatta sailing. Visiting boats have to make a real effort to get there – and that effort is appreciated by the local club. For visiting South Isles yoles, the experience is heightened by the fraught trip on and off the ferry, which necessitates everyone working together. The following description from Maurice in his inimitable style and peppered with Orcadian dialect gives us a glimpse of the experience.]

WINDY WESTRAY by Maurice Davidson

What planning and wark[78] goes into the Westray Regatta! Though you'd never know as the day quietly unfolds, layer after layer.

Before the sun is out of bed, we're rowing out to our yoles moored in Hamnavoe and pull them into the slip. Trailers are dooked[79] into the sea, yoles pulled in and the steel frames pulled out again, now laden with wood and sail. Magic.

The soft curves of these boats look even better out of water. A few words and cars purr, we all roll away in convoy to Kirkwall, with the glimmers of a thin sun peeking ower sleepy Orphir hills.

It's all monster drumming engines and harsh shouts under the enormous jaws of the North Isles ferry.

- Get in line! – Ower here! – Bloody yoles, fer too heavy. – Git those dinghies oot o' the way! – Watch oot! – and a few curses as we manhandle old style all the sailing boats into the car deck, with not a car in sight just for today.

A colourful cargo of curves is onboard as the sun rises for breakfast. The crowd of yellow and orange whiskered faces all laughing with anticipation and shouting good-natured insults, retreat for mince rolls and warm coffee below. Two hours of banter, playing I spy with all the skerries, and we slip into Pierowall – for our non roll-off[80] day at the races.

The fun begins, as some of the dinghies are launched off the rear ramp, straight into the harbour. The rest of the boats are hoisted skywards on rope slings with the ferry crane, just as in old days everything was. Including the kye skittering[81] out over folk in wide circles! Eager hands then heave yoles round to the slipway.

Communal activity forms a community. If you don't all lend a hand, it won't happen. And it does, in Westray and the other isles. Townies have become a bit too independent, with machines for everything so no longer need to rely on their neighbours. Community activity is a forgotten art, certainly not seen in city commercial chambers for a while, usually dissolving into finger-pointing blame!

A flutter of sails in the bright breeze, tea and hot snacks at the fish factory briefing. And we're all off. Guns crack! Races begin.

---

[78] work
[79] ducked

[80] No roll-on roll-off ferry here. Competing boats, on their trailers, are craned off.
[81] Cattle excreting

South Isles yole Sumato hoisted off the North Isles ferry at Pierowall, Westray on its trailer.
Enthusiastic Westray sailors then help the crew to push and launch her at their slip, 2016.

Tight lines of goose white wings suddenly fly apart in all directions across the bay. Boats zig and zag and slowly creep away from each other, as the fast focus and the slow enjoy a laugh.

Those who read the wind – a strong force 5 breeze, gusting 6 – started slower with reefed sails, but keep on going! Half the fleet capsize or retire at half-mast. The huge glistening lifeboat swamps us all as she cruises slowly past, full of crowds and cameras. Carnival in the North.

An hour and a half of tense silence and sweat, and we survive race one. Wet and smiling. More welcome tea and pizza slices, amongst the warm fog of steaming partans bathing in their huge cauldrons. Then we're off again. They're organized up here! Time and tide – and the ferry - wait for no man.

All the yoles and skiffs squeeze in towards the pier at the crack of the gun. The banter is pretty sharp too!

Whit's aal this? - STAARBORD! - they're gaen on aboot[82]! An – GIMME WATTER! – when you are all sailing on the stuff?

Dinghies do that when slower but heavier yoles crunch them along barnacled piers or into fat orange buoys. It's a hard life in the fast lane.

The peace as we sail round is a relief, after all the clatter and jostle at the start. Fields of yellow barley and luscious green silage sigh with their ripe cargo, as invisible hands bend their heads in dark unison. Our mast also bends, as bulging sails race with the white clouds scudding across blue sky. A great sail amongst white snorting horses in the bay.

Suddenly we're back in the hubbub of humanity, near the pier and the start line again. Shouts of – WHERE'S THE FINISH LINE? and - GIMME WAATER! echo again.

After a few small knocks and scrapes, sails are stowed, yoles are slipped and hoisted back onboard. Quiet is restored. It must be tea time.

Lines of salt-stained eyes all head straight across the whiter than white sands, no tacking into the wind now, to the bulging marquee tent that disguises an ancient Pierowall Hotel. A few pints to dissolve the taste of the sea, encourages more crack and jostle. Squalls of banter and verbal blows harder than any breeze in our azure bay.

Then the main event of the day: Tea!

You will never believe the spread of colour and texture and smells, masked by the tent, that greet you in the queue for food! It's too much for hungry salts, and half the line munch away and then fill the plates up again as we slowly progress. A food carnival of fish and meat, salmon and partan[83], chicken and fresh vegetables. Soups and desserts. And oh! Those desserts – sweet and alluring puddings, dripping chocolate éclairs and profiteroles! Fresh red strawberry and cream tarts seduce the hapless sailors, steaming puddings and cakes and more.

---

[82] Going on about

[83] Brown crab

Three smaller 15 foot lugsail yoles from Papay, sail in the 2016 Westray Regatta. Originally for fishing, these were built by the Miller family and are still enthusiastically sailed by them.

If you're not packed to the gunnels after this tented feast, then you haven't lived! Everyone is silenced by the feed. Lips are licked and bellies groan.

Cups are awarded as a sideline; the real awards are given in the bar – a cutting crack and a jovial jest. Trophies are filled with some awful mixtures and emptied with gasps and grimaces! Somehow a few more foaming pints are squeezed in as last orders are shouted – the ferry is leaving, time to go.

We stumble across the bay again and fall onboard. Ropes are unleashed and they're off. Most off to sleep for a couple of hours till Kirkwall.

What a great day!

Thanks to all for their organization and the helping hands. The sailing clubs, the ferry hands, the folk helping at the pier and slip and rescue boats (and lifeboat).

But the real thanks must go to all those lovely lassies who cooked and served with huge smiles, all that wonderful food! Fresh, tasty, and jist what a salty stomach needs. It's worth going to the regatta just for this culinary extravaganza. The Brighton flower show for colourful food! And all for a fiver. Unbelievable. Unbeatable.

For those of us who stayed on, there was a whirling dance in the hall followed by more waltzing among yachts and gin palaces that night.

Force 10 winds kept us prisoner for another day (or was it two?) as we munched our way through the best hotel menu in Orkney. Every kind of fish - and meat – that you can think of, friendly chat in the bar and the cheapest good wine you'll not find in Kirkwall. Keps aff[84] to the Pierowall Hotel! Again.

After two stormy days of sand dune walks and old stone ruins in sunshine – we finally sailed back to Kirkwall in record time. Faster than the auld steamy *m.v. Sigurd*.

Just a grand trip.

---

[84] Hats off

2010 sail visit to Stromness of Sgoth Jubilee from Neiss (Ness) Lewis, Hebrides, 100 miles West.
She is 21 feet long with a large, single dipping lugsail. Sailed back in September in 22 hours.

2017 Longhope regatta yoles all tied up for a well earned rest next to the pier.
Nearest is Lotte, then Lily, Sumato, Gremsa, Mohican and Family Pride.

2008 Longhope Regatta, Ian McFadyen's South Isles spreet (sprit) sailed yole Emma being chased by Gremsa in a close race. You don't have to sail fast to get exciting races.

Waterwitch with Lily just behind and Gremsa in front at the starting line of the 2019 Stromness Regatta. All three South Isles yoles are spreet (sprit) sail rigged.

2010 Westray Regatta with large, slim North Isles yole Ivy, built c.1930 in Deerness. Small North Isles skiffs all racing fast with Bermudan rigs. Lily in the background with gunter rig.

Section 6 Building and Restoring Orkney Yoles

[The first article in this section, superbly illustrated by photographs taken by Richard Wilson, gives a fascinating insight into how a yole is built, even for the layman with no knowledge of boat building. See the glossary at the end of the book for explanations of other parts of the boat not highlighted in the photographs.]

BUILDING AN 18 FOOT SOUTH ISLES ORKNEY YOLE by Ian B Richardson

Traditionally, Orkney yoles were built 'by eye', resulting in a great variety of boats from a range of boatbuilders, while still conforming to the characteristic 'double-ended' design with 10 or 11 planks, clinker-built of larch on an oak frame, and dimensions generally in the region of 18 feet overall length, beam of about 7ft 4 inches and depth of about 3ft 4 inches.

In recent years, I have built a number of yoles using drawings made by naval architect Dennis Davidson in 2002 from measurements taken from a 'grand old lady', *Emma*, which is an 18ft South Isles Orkney yole built on Flotta around 1910 - and which is still sailing, based in Longhope. One of these yoles was the *Lily*, which was built in 2008 for the Orkney Yole Association.

When building yoles, I still use larch planks ($7/16$ inch) for the skin, but the traditional oak for the keel, stem and stern have been replaced by Opepe, a very durable marine hardwood. Copper nails are used for the main fastenings.

Clinker-built wooden boats are built 'the right way up', and so the building starts with a simple building jig in position holding the keel, to which the stem is joined using a 'housed' half-checked joint and the stern with a full half-checked one. The joints are fastened using copper nails. Stem and stern 'knees' are then bolted on to provide strength to these important joints.

stem   knee   keel

Before the planking can begin, apron pieces are shaped and fastened to both stem and stern posts to form the plank 'landings'. A 'hog' is prepared and attached to the top of the keel, before bevelling along the rebate lines and using small, approx. 10-inch, temporary moulds along the hog to give the required bevel for attaching the garboards.

The nailing positions are marked on the hog, in this case at 4½ inch centres, alternately for nailing the garboard to the hog and the garboard to a timmer (when they have been fitted), giving a timmer position of 9-inch centres. It is advisable to do a bit of forward planning here to ensure that the moulds to be used for the build are set against a timmer position and not where you need to nail the planks together.

One garboard is always shaped, flat at the bottom along the line of the keel and curved at the top so that it is broader at both stem and stern, at about 7 inches, than it is in the middle, at about 4 inches. It is then loose fitted to confirm a good fit, before being removed and used as a template to produce an identical garboard for the other side of the boat. This is standard procedure for all planks to ensure the two sides of the boat are identical. The garboards are then fitted along the keel hog, as well as to both the stem and the stern aprons, using silicon bronze ring-nails and silicon bronze screws.

Building moulds are then placed in position along the hog and the plank widths are marked on them. In order to calculate the required plank width, the distances between the top of the garboard and the desired sheer line can be divided by 10, if the final planned total number of planks is eleven on each side.

stem   garboard   small moulds

A second plank is then shaped by taking a spiling board (frequently a rejected plank from a previous build using the same plank thickness) and placing it along the garboard with an overlap. From the inside, this board is marked along the top edge of the garboard. The spiling board is then placed on the selected piece of timber for the new plank, and the line transferred to it, forming the bottom edge of the second plank. From the moulds, the width of the new plank is taken, remembering for clinker-built boats that you need to add the amount of desired overlap (landing) of the planks, which is usually twice the thickness of the plank - in this case that gives an additional ⅞ inch. A spiling batten is then used to join up the marks. When satisfied with the shape, the plank is cut and dressed, before being loosely fitted. If happy with that, once again a duplicate second plank is made for the other side of the boat, as described before.

The second planks are then fitted, using clamps to hold them to the garboard, before the nail holes are marked, in line with those on the garboard, and bored. Copper nails with roves are then clenched to provide a very strong bond between the two planks. This nailing, or riveting, is a one-man job.

Spiling, or templating, the next plank (strake)

apron full moulds

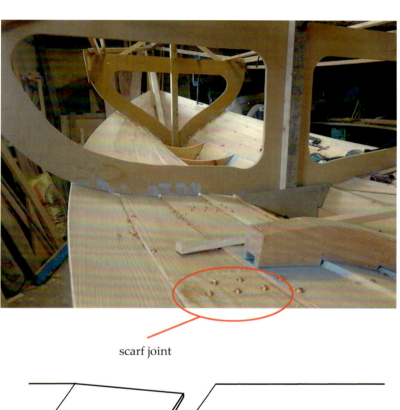

scarf joint

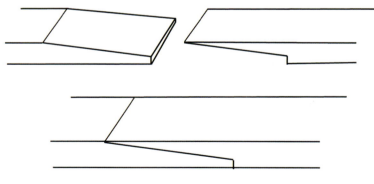

Diagram – scarf joint

However, for the remaining planks, a single board the full length of the boat would require a very wide piece of timber, to allow for the curves and bends required along the length of the boat, and would be very cumbersome to work with, so two pieces of plank can be used, joining them with a scarf joint. The rule for the preferred length of a scarf overlap is 6 to 8 times the thickness of the plank, so this results in a scarf of between 3½ and 4 inches. To provide strength to the build, the scarf joints should normally be towards the middle section of the boat, but also need to be staggered. A degree of steaming of the planks is also generally needed on virtually all the remaining planks in order to ease their fitting without stressing the wood – or the builder!

Planking finished

With the planking up to the sheer line, the moulds can be removed and the inside of the boat should be primed before any further construction work takes place - as this might be the only coat of paint that some parts of the boat ever get!

The Nordic style!

Temporary battens to retain the width of the boat when timmers are being fitted.

"bridges"

Inside of the boat painted and ready for timmers to be fitted

Before undertaking the next task of fitting the timmers (ribs), however, it is a good idea to fasten temporary battens across the top of the boat in order to prevent the planned beam increasing when the timmers are being fitted.

Every second timmer to be fitted will run from the sheer line to the garboard at the bottom. Alternate timmers, however, will be fitted from one sheer line to the opposite one, with 'bridges' set above the hog to provide additional support and strength to the framework.

The timmer positions can now be marked on the planks and the nail holes carefully bored into the skin. Copper nails are driven into the planks, but not through them, making the boat look a bit like a porcupine. Fitting of the timmers is a two-man job with one inside the boat and one outside.

Traditionally oak was, and still can be, used for the timmers. However, if it is difficult to get good quality oak which won't split, larch works just as well. The timmers are first steamed, then quickly pressed into place by the person inside the boat, while the person outside the boat drives the nails into each timmer, locking it in place. This process requires good planning, teamwork, precision and speed in order to be successful – and can be 'hot work'!

Fitting steamed timmers is 'hot work'!

When the timmers are all in place, the nails need to be clenched. This is another two-man job with one person outside the boat holding the nail heads, and the other inside the boat fitting the rove, before cutting the excess nail, leaving a short stub, which is then hammered to clench it over the rove.

After this, gunwales, stringers, and fore and aft knees (breasthooks or hunnyspots) are fitted, all providing strength and integrity to the boat structure. On yoles, stringers are usually set at about 7 inches below the gunwales and provide supports for the seats (thafts), which will be additionally secured to the gunwales with centred vertical knees. Mast steps (one or two generally, depending on the rig to be used) and floor boards come next, although it's always worth thinking about getting the floorboards in as soon as practicable, as they provide a stable platform to work from. Seats (thafts), as required, and a Samson post, if appropriate, can also be done now.

Gunwales, stringers and decking supports fitted.

Decking finished, mast steps, floorboards and seats (thafts) fitted.

If the boat is to have any decking, appropriate support beams can now also be fitted, before the decking itself.

Then, of course, a suitable rudder and tiller need to be fashioned, as well as any required masts and spars, depending on the rig to be used. I find Douglas Fir to be the best for masts and spars, and I normally recommend constructing hollow masts for strength and flexibility.

Tiller and rudder fashioned and fitted, and waterline marked.

Port side newly painted

Painting complete

Finally, you might be interested to know how long it takes to build a typical 18-foot Orkney yole. Having checked my work diary for building the yole *Lily*, I can confirm that it took me a total of 667 hours, not counting the painting, which was undertaken, on a voluntary basis, by OYA members.

Ready to launch!

Lily, newly launched

[Sheena's next article tells us how the OYA went about the process of raising money for and commissioning local boatbuilder Ian Richardson to build the Lily. We hear more from Ian Richardson in the following article about his career as a boatbuilder and how he learned the necessary skills. The Lily has featured prominently in our articles on Regattas and is in many of our photographs. With both gunter and sprit-sail rigs available, she has proved a very versatile craft and is an ideal boat to pass on the traditional sailing skills to our local youngsters.]

BUILDING THE *LILY* by Sheena Taylor

In 2006 Robbie Drever, Orkney Yole Association President at the time, wanted to build a yole to be owned by the Association and pressed the committee into agreement, adding, "It'll be called the *Lily*."

The proposed project also included a flattie (a local form of flat-bottomed dinghy), two suits of sails and sailing rigs - spritsail and gunter rigs – an outboard motor, road trailer and fifteen buoyancy aids for children.

An application to the Heritage Lottery Fund ("HLF") was submitted by the Association's secretary, drawing on information supplied by members. The secretary reported that, if HLF liked the project, they would grant up to 57% of the cost. Consequently, the application form was very demanding and detailed. The project had to be justified by demonstrating its heritage and educational value to the local community, as well as projecting costs and a timetable for completion.

A project management team was set up consisting of:

Project Manager	Dennis Davidson, CEng MRINA. (Dennis was in Helensburgh and Len Wilson provided liaison.)
Boatbuilder	Ian Richardson.
Secretary	Len Wilson.
Webmaster	Richard Wilson.
Finance Manager	Pat Tulloch.

The opening paragraph of the Yole Association's submission to HLF justifying the building of a yole on traditional lines ran as follows:

It will create a new public interest and awareness of an important part of Orkney's economic and social history, providing the opportunity for Orcadians of all ages to learn about, and participate in, the local seafaring activities of their forefathers, in boats which are unique to these islands and require specialist sailing skills. For many it will be the start of a lifelong pastime and interest. We propose to build a replica sailing yole and a Stromness Flattie rowing tender to accompany it. With them we will operate a yole experience programme for schoolchildren and the general public.

To demonstrate competence to see the project through successfully, the Association was able to list in its membership one naval architect, four boat-builders, three master mariners, several seamen, a solicitor, and several lifeboat men, including a coxswain and a retired coxswain. This was thought to be an impressive array of expertise for such a project.

That opinion was evidently shared by the Heritage Lottery Fund committee in reaching their decision to award a grant of £22,700. The Orkney Yole Association added around £2,500 as well as non-cash contributions of more than £14,000 in the form of research and drawing up plans, supervisory costs, website training, volunteer effort, recording and archiving, publicity, and running the Association's first educational event. Boatbuilding plans and photographs were lodged with the Orkney Library Archive.

The HLF grant was approved in March 2007 and the keel laid later in the year. *Lily* was launched on 10th May 2008, with a public naming ceremony at the Navigation School's pier.

With assistance from Stromness Primary School staff and members of the Council's Education Department, who provided guidance on risk assessment and other safety procedures, Stromness Primary 7 pupils were taken for a sail experience on 3rd June with a second session on the 24th. That activity was followed by a public sailing event from the Broad Noust at Stromness Museum on 20th July.

Since then, Orkney Yole Association and Navigation Department staff have repeated and extended that programme annually (with the sole exception of 2020, due to Covid-19), with *Lily* joined by privately owned boats, their skippers and crews.

The tight sailing in matched South Isles yoles Helga and Solwen, broad reach in Stromness harbour. Traditionally the large and high gunter rigs were used only for regattas.

[Ian Richardson was a boatbuilder in Stromness, Orkney for many years. Since this interview was conducted, he has retired but continues to sail his yole, the Solwen, in Stromness, and is a trustee of the Orkney Yole Association. He has built many of the yoles listed on our register of seaworthy yoles, some of which have found their way across Europe, and is regularly consulted by local yole owners on how to maintain their boats.]

IAN RICHARDSON'S BOATBUILDING CAREER - interview by Maurice Davidson

How did it all start? I was born in Edinburgh and grew up in Leeds. Growing up, I rowed boats and I sketched boats and made models of boats. I was interested in both boats and textiles, and boats won. My family then moved to Arran and there were more wooden clinker boats for me to play with. My family knew of Ewing McGruer, a well-known boat designer from nearby Clynder, on the Clyde. So, a family friend asked Mr McGruer who he would recommend for me to contact for boat building training. He had no hesitation in recommending James Anderson (known as Pia), a Stromness boatbuilder, who was then building 36-foot long wooden clinker and carvel fishing boats, which were grant-funded by the Highlands and Islands Development Board.

When did you come to Orkney? I finally met Pia at Ewing McGruer's funeral and he agreed for me to come to work and train with him in Stromness. He told me I would also learn to swear! So up I came, on my 18th birthday in 1966, to learn to build wooden boats at his first yard, a collection of old black corrugated tin and stone sheds, on what is now the Navigation School pier.

I started in time to see him launch a new creel boat, the Three Boys, built for local ferryman, Ginger Brown, side-on over the old stone pier. My first job was endlessly threading steel bolts and hammering round heads, all by hand. After one year, Pia sent me to do a 10 months' boatbuilding training course at Southampton college.

In 1970, after two and a half more years at Pia's new Ness yard, learning more about timber fishing boats, I left to work for the high-end McGruer yacht yard, on the Clyde. Dennis Davidson[85] was the naval architect there. I spent two years there, learning a finer form of timber boatbuilding, with lots of attention to detail and finish.

Then I left for a desk job with Lloyd's Register of Shipping, for two years' training to be a Lloyd's surveyor, and spent my time checking that the designs and construction of boats were in accordance with the regulations.

After one year, 25% VAT was put on the price of new leisure boats in UK, which caused a collapse in the market.

I was made redundant because, knowledgeable and experienced as I was in wooden boats, I lacked the required experience of glass reinforced plastic.

---

[85] Dennis Davidson is the brother of Maurice Davidson, the current commodore of OYA and has contributed one of the articles in section 1

Ian Richardson, boatbuilder, clamping on the spiling, or template, for the fourth strake of OYA's new South Isles yole Lily, September 2007. Two of three mould frames are shown.

I came back to Pia's yard, now run by a manager, and worked on a large 54-foot wooden trawler for a year. Then, in 1975, I decided that it would give me more satisfaction to build smaller wooden boats on my own. So, I started off in my small garden shed at York House, on Hillside Road, Stromness. J & W McKay's boatyard, run by Arthur Sinclair and building mahogany clinker dinghies for leisure fishing, was still employing three folk near Stromness' North pier at that time.

My first boat was a small 12-foot clinker dinghy for a customer in Mallaig, who then ordered one more. The dinghies had to be set on their sides to get out of my shed and then pulled through the field to the back track in order to take them away.

That summer I trailered another dinghy around Scotland to advertise my work, as far as Edinburgh. I got more dinghy orders and the ball started rolling, slowly. A trip to Southampton boat show brought in more dinghy work. But it was hard times and every pound mattered. In 1981, I got an order for a 21-foot, transom stern fishing boat, so I bought the end half of the old Egg Packing Station, which I still occupy today, but with double the space.

This clinker fishing boat must have been well liked by the Johnshaven fishermen, south of Aberdeen, as another boat was soon ordered. I started to get a good name for larger fishing boats. This soon led to building two other similar boats: George Sinclair's *Strowa*, a 38-foot carvel, creel boat, then the *Silver Wave*, at 35-foot.

The largest clinker boat I built was in 1984, a full 47-foot Viking longship, ordered by a South coast yard that made boats for the film industry. A Viking film was on the go, filmed in Lyme Regis. I last saw the Viking ship sailing onto a Two Ronnies television sketch.

In the 1980s I had got my first yole order for a sheep-carrying boat. The Hebridean owner had an old Orkney yole which he used to sail or tow out to some isles off the West coast to load and offload his sheep. He needed a new yole. I built a 20-foot beach yole, a beamy 9 feet wide to hold loads of sheep, the same purpose as the yole was developed for in Orkney. He would bring the yole into the beach at high water, lean her over and out would jump the sheep. The reverse process took place at low water when loading up.

By the early 1990s I was fitting out more large steel and fibreglass fishing boats funded by Highlands and Islands Development Board grants, and built the new steel shed next door. This period ended up in mid-1996, when we fitted out the new GRP Foula ferry, for Shetland. After this large boat there was little work to be had so I paid off my men and decided to work on my own, concentrating on wood work to get more satisfaction.

I built my first Westray skiff, the *Auk*, and took her off to the Southampton boat show in 1994. Ian Outred, a well-known small boat builder and sailor, subsequently bought her and she got good press reports in many magazines. This led to an order for the 16.5-foot yole *Halle*, now in Edinburgh. I took the *Halle* to Portsoy boat festival and she was well liked, a new curved shape to most folk.

I then built the similar *Philabin*, which went to the Republic of Ireland after being exhibited in Southampton, and has recently returned to sail in Longhope.

2017. Ian Richardson's yard with a brelkie (full bilged) Stroma-Flotta rebuild Waterwitch (left) and Ian's newest lean, fast Emma-type yole. The steam box at the front is for bending strakes.

In 1994, Willie Tulloch wanted a replacement for his old *Emma*, a South Isles yole now back in Longhope. Dennis Davidson took measurements to make the shape accurate and we created three template moulds at quarter sections. By 1995 a new Orkney yole with gunter rig sails was launched. The *Helga* can still be seen sailing in Stromness.

The *Frances*, an 18-foot, three-sailed spritsail yole, was built by me in 1996 and taken to several shows to advertise my skills. After some reshaping to make her curves more authentic, she finally took to the sea in 1998 and recently headed off, without masts and sails, to Flotta, now used as a motorised fishing yole.

After more commercial work fitting out large steel and GRP fishing boats, I suddenly got a huge order while sailing the Frances at the 2002 Great Glen raid. The owner liked the look of the Frances and promptly unfurled plans for a larger yole, a 34-foot sixareen[86]-shaped, clinker yacht, the *Io Contesta*, built for West coast cruising. This very curvaceous double-ender was craned into Stromness marina in 2004. She later went to Crinan but has now returned to Stromness.

Meanwhile, after repairing Eric Linklater's old 21-foot elliptical sterned yole, I thought I could build a new yole in this easy going and graceful shape. And so, the 18-foot *Eve* took shape, with the same yole lines as the *Helga* below water, but with an inboard rudder, small engine and long, smoothed out stern above water. Launched in 2007, she appeared at several boat shows, was much admired and eventually sold South.

The Orkney Yole Association wanted a yole to encourage young folk to sail these seaworthy traditional boats, and raised funding to build one. The *Lily*, similar to the *Helga*, with side decks and 100 lbs of lead in her keel, was launched with a fanfare in Stromness harbour in 2008. She has since sailed in all Orkney regattas, helmed by a variety of local folk, and usually coming in first. Allie Kirkpatrick, from Kirkwall, took her to his heart and sailed in a winning streak for many years.

Further orders for these elliptical sterned yoles produced the *Wonne* in 2011, bound for Holland and then Lake Geneva, Switzerland. Then came the *Lady Hamilton* in 2012, which headed off to France.

My next Orkney South Isles yole, the *Solwen*, sailed into Stromness harbour in 2012 and gives her sister *Lily* a look at her stern, sometimes.

In 2016, I built another Emma-type South Isles yole, this time with gunwales only and no side deck, and a revised thwart layout providing seats along the side. She is ready to sail and has been to the Southampton boat show. At the same time, I finished the restoration of the old, completely rebuilt, South Isles yole *Waterwitch*, still sailed in Stromness.

---

[86] A boat used by Shetland islanders. Its shape is more akin to the traditional concept of a Viking longship. They were rowed by a crew of six – hence the name.

The elliptic stern of Ian Richardson's last yole built in 2019, or so he said on retirement. The lines are based on the Lily, with extended stern ellipse, to gain speed in strong winds.

These 18-foot Emma-type yoles now cost more than double the cost of the first one I built, with inflation. I now charge £20,000 for the hull and hollow mast that I now make, and £23,000 when fitted with gunter sails.

I used to keep the construction very traditional, with oak frame, timbers and larch strakes, but have found opepe hardwood more stable for the main frame, and steam larch timbers now. The yole shape and construction is as traditional as I can make it, and this has been my trademark. Folk South are generally very impressed with a traditional boat designed to handle the tides and seas up here, with the yole's unique shape.

Finally, I have a new 19-foot elliptical sterned yole on the stocks right now, with small 10HP diesel engine and gunter sail rig, named *Nonameyet*. This is my last yole before retiring! I have been building wooden boats for 52 years now and my body tells me to retire now while I am in good health.

For the future? Jeff Mackie is now building boats here, having been trained in Lowestoft. He has just completed a Westray skiff and he is now repairing a Hoy dinghy, our bread-and-butter work. There are very few small wooden boat builders in Scotland now.

Of course, I may build one more yole, just to keep my skills sharp. It's in the blood now!

Norrie Mowat's buoyant, round hulled Stroma yole hauled up for the winter in Stromness. He used her for lobster creels in the summers, 1969.

Ian Richardson's last traditional yole, a sleek bilged Emma-type South Isles yole on the stocks in his Stromness yard, 2017.

[Ken Sutherland's article below describes how a few beers in Longhope led to a surprise decision to restore a yole which was over 100 years old. The man who carried out her restoration also restored several other yoles mentioned elsewhere in this book. Read on to learn the Sumato's history and how she introduced an ex Merchant Navy man to the joys of sailing – capsizes included!]

THE RESTORATION OF THE *SUMATO* by Captain Ken Sutherland

The Past

The *Sumato* was built by John Duncan of South Ronaldsay around 1892, as the Jeanette, and registered for fishing with lines on 12th July 1893 with the registration number K494. Its master was George Dunnett, Windwick, South Ronaldsay. She was re-registered by her new owner William Annal, Ballgreen, South Ronaldsay and re-named *Sumato* on 3rd July 1936.

William Mowatt, the blacksmith on South Ronaldsay, told me, a few years before he died on 16th September 2016 at the age of 91, that he thought she had been built at Herston, South Ronaldsay and that she was taken to Brims, Melsetter, Hoy by someone who sailed on whaling ships but whose name he couldn't remember.

On 7th September 1938, she was re-registered by Daniel and Thomas Kirkpatrick, Brims, Melsetter, Hoy. Daniel (Dan) Kirkpatrick subsequently became coxswain of the Longhope lifeboat from 1955 to 1969. The family used the *Sumato* as the working yole and the *Family Pride* was the regatta yole.

On 15th August 1969, she was re-registered by Garry Kirkpatrick, Brimsness, Brims, Melsetter, Hoy. Garry is the son of Dan. At some point she had an engine fitted, possibly by the Kirkpatricks in 1938, and was used for creeling.

Restoration

In 2005, during one of my frequent visits to Longhope, I met up with Alex Norquoy at Terry and Ethel Joyce's house. Alex asked me if I would be interested in restoring a yole which was lying by the side of a field beside Davy Learmonth's house at Wyng, South Walls (see photograph on facing page). After a few beers, I expressed an interest and we all duly went and inspected her. She was in a pretty poor condition, with grass growing through the bottom of her and, really, she was ready for the bonfire. However, after a few more beers and with a bit of encouragement from Alex, I agreed to have her restored. With this decision, my life would never be the same again.

I then approached John A Mowat of Brims (John A) and he agreed to carry out the restoration. The project was worked on as time permitted and the detailed and careful restoration took about three years and involved around 750 hours of work. I was absolutely delighted with how the boat, with a length of 19 feet and a beam of 8 feet, turned out. John A made a beautiful job of her and it is a testimony to his skills that you would not know where the original timber construction ended and the new started. John A is a self-taught boat restorer based in Brims, Hoy. Other boats he has carefully restored include: *Family Pride, Aerial, Pansy, Emma, Irene* and *Chrisie*.

Sumato, lying in the field before her restoration

The mast, boom and gaff were built by Ian Richardson, the Stromness boatbuilder and the sails supplied by Leitch Sails of Tarbert.

As well as being the catalyst for the restoration of the *Sumato*, Alex (along with John A) has restored his own yole, the *Pansy*. In addition, he was also instrumental in getting the redundant Longhope lifeboat shed restored and established as the Longhope Lifeboat Museum.

New beginnings

Whilst I had qualified as a foreign going master and served 25 years in the Merchant Navy, apart from sailing a lifeboat with a dipping lug-sail in the mid 1960s in Wellington harbour, New Zealand, I had never learned to sail a sailing boat. However, in 2008, after John A had sailed the *Sumato* up to Stromness marina from Longhope, Willie Tulloch gave me a very quick lesson in how to rig her and a few quick lessons in how to sail her round Stromness harbour. I was then, allegedly, 'good to go'. I didn't fit an outboard motor since I wanted to learn how to berth and depart the pontoon just with sail. Although this was a great learning curve, I did become fed up of being towed in when becalmed with the midges and being towed off the shore after 'gently' blowing ashore when getting the tacking manoeuvres wrong.

To avoid further embarrassment, an outboard motor was duly fitted after the first two seasons of sailing. Being the great tutor that he is, Willie accompanied me on the first few regattas, and I quickly realised that this is where you really learn how to sail. Stromness regatta was my first one and, whilst attempting to tack round a buoy in the middle of Hoy Sound, the jam cleat for the mainsail became seriously jammed and couldn't be released quickly enough to avoid capsizing. I will never forget the awe of watching the sea pouring in over the starboard gunwale before it sank under the surface with the rest of the boat quickly following. I had previously been assured that it was impossible to capsize such a wide-beamed yole – not true.

As we were floating with our lifejackets fully inflated, Willie reckoned I looked like one of those booby birds with its cheeks fully crammed with fish – not funny. The other crew, David Bews and Arthur Robson, will never forget that day. Strangely enough, neither will Willie or I. Luckily, Arthur had stowed a couple of buoys under the bow decking and this kept the *Sumato* afloat until she was towed to the Ness slipway. Otherwise, she would have sunk like a stone.

I soon learnt which yole to keep well clear of at the start of regattas as we usually ended up 'making contact'. Willie never bats an eyelid but he does mutter quietly under his breath.

At one Holm regatta, whilst trying to get ourselves into the ideal position for 'the off', we ended up running aground on a skerry to the east of the pier. Helpfully, John Lawrence jumped in immediately and was able to rock us off and we were away. Not to win, alas. It was no consolation that a few of the pierhead worthies told me that everyone from the local sailing club had run aground there at some point in their sailing career.

I also remember one Longhope regatta where she was leaking like a sieve, as I had only put her in the water a few days before the regatta and the timbers had still not 'taken up'. My stepson, Kenny Low, as well as looking after the jib sheets, had to man the pump all the way round the course and that was his first regatta. Two years later, he still complains that his arm is not quite right yet. They don't make them like they used to.

I have had great fun over the last 11 or 12 years sailing the *Sumato* on a Thursday evening with other Yole Association members and joining in the annual regattas which are held throughout Orkney in July. My favourites are the Longhope and Westray regattas: not to be missed! So, after nearly 130 years, the *Jeanette / Sumato* continues to bring as much enjoyment to the present owner as I am sure she did to the original and subsequent owners before me. I certainly do not regret the decision to have the *Sumato* restored; in particular, I don't regret enjoying those few beers with Alex.

Fully restored *Sumato*

John A and Alex Norquoy working together

187　South Isles yole Sumato in full flight, goose-winged, running down past the Peter Skerry buoy en route to the Holm Regatta, 2016.

The Helga reaching at full speed in a force 5 wind at the Holm Regatta 2011. Note how she sits down in the large wave trough at the stern, requiring weight moved forward.

South Isles yole Helga, gunter rigged, with a crew of young and old enjoying the good wind, 2006.

A fleet of South Isles yoles all with three spreet (sprit) sails racing in Stromness harbour between the wars.

Section 7 Out at sea on a Yole

[This final section contains a selection of stories of sailing trips on a yole, most contributed by Maurice Davidson in his own Orcadian dialect as he originally wrote them for publication in The Orcadian. They take us off Hoy, out into the Pentland Firth, round South Ronaldsay and around Eday, mainly in fine weather; but they culminate in a dramatic storm in the Firth in 1959. They are stories to savour on a winter's night, to inspire us for our own voyages in the coming summer. In the first of these articles below, Maurice takes us off Hoy to fish for ling.]

A DAY AT THE AULD MAN by Maurice Davidson

Every year we try to sail out for a fish or two off the Face of Hoy, to fill the freezers for winter. What better taste than a fresh fry of fish, rolled in oatmeal, with new tatties and butter.

Despite gloom and doom over fish stocks there still seems to be a fair few good size saithe, lythe, cod and ling inshore here, hiding away from trawlers, among rocks and creels. Maybe shoals of fish just wait here, in the shadows of Rora, for the *m.v. Hamnavoe* and its passengers to throw up their auld food - or maybe they jist sook[87] creel bait? Who said fish have no brains?

Fishing is just an excuse for a sail in our yole amid the most spectacular coastal scenery in Britain. Fast tides, huge cliffs, geos, rolling hills, seabirds and, of course, the Auld Man and the Pentland Firth.

Willie rigs up the *Helga*, a modern gunter-sailed yole in our new Stromness marina - sheltered, convenient and quick. We take a slower, more sea-kindly, journey to our yole – the *Gremsa* – moored off Flaas' Pier in the Sooth End, next to the museum.

We gather oars and rowlocks from our sail store on the pier. A peedie[88] stone house where two families used to eke out a living from the sea. Two small rooms 10-foot square, one up one down, with a couple of small windows keeping an eye on the sea. A young family with kids upstairs - under a cold, damp flag roof, huddled round their tiny open fire. Auld folk grumbling with the rheumatics downstairs in their box bed, with all the bustle of cooking and washing around them. Glad to get out for a quiet pipe of Back twist on the grey weathered pier bench. Just right to speer[89] zulus and yoles tacking out into the ebb. We must sail out with the tide, too.

Our auld flattie is a bit gizened up[90] after being stored in our garden shed for 38 years! But a couple of baths in saltwater has tightened up the timber strakes. Set our fishing gear in, flask of tea, biscuits and waterproofs? – the golden sun burns so well this year, we need oilskins for shade!

---

[87] suck
[88] small
[89] look closely at
[90] dried up

The remains of the motor yole *Spray* lie in a noust adjacent to the sail-house at Skaefea on Graemsay. Her last owner Ronnie Mowat from Ramray used the boat to transport farm supplies from Stromness each week and to catch fish and lobsters off Hoy and Graemsay. The yole was moored afloat at Skaefea or Sandside except during the winter when it was worked off the beach at Skaefea. A fore-deck and two extra strakes appear to have been added later to heighten the yole. The *Spray*, which was the last working yole on the island, has lain ashore since about 1980.

Thanks to Neil Mowat for information on the yole's name and history.

Painter unravelled from the rusty iron hoop, and a small kick rumbles her down this wedge of stone cheese into the sea. No nile[91] to forget on this Graemsay flattie!

You live history here, rowing out amongst salt-worn gables that have seen storm and seagulls these past 300 years. How many anxious old faces peering out at white scud and surf, joyous screams of kids leaping off warm stone into bright summer brine, silent baskets of gulping haddock dragged up the slip and young lovers kissing on these quiet stone stages. And it all still lives on.

Rigging the yole is like harnessing a horse. One minute, it's lying content in a field; then, suddenly, raffles of rope, rattling gear, flapping canvas and curses and laughter of anticipation. Then silence as all goes tight, barnacled buoys are unleashed – and we're away! Slowly and silently at first, till shadows of the piers are thrown off. Then the first dark wind spatters on the sea, whisks us into brilliant fresh crystal, round Ness, and red sails dive into the last o' the ebb.

Low soft curves roll westwards along the verdant shores of Graemsay and our lovely golf course. A conveyor belt of current whisks the yole into its own breeze out west, past three whitewashed sentinels of Hoy Sound, their eyes blinded by fire in the sky.

Our peedie yole seems so insignificant off Selwick's jagged teeth, amongst huge whale shadows of Hoy. We try for a lythe off rusty boilers, gutted from the *Strathelliot* when she ripped the Bow Rock around the time I was born. The golden shoals of fish laugh at us in crystal seas – the breeze stutters to a halt.

Our wee engine booms out across gaunt echoes in Ooting's dark geos, as cries of the *Leicester City*'s hardened trawlermen, up in the rigging, still go unheard through the fog of time. Another red rust gravestone, warning us to keep off these riven shoals.

We quickly flash our rainbow warriors into fish baskets, as mackerel shimmer to a quiet grave. The Kame's sandy depths have fed us well in sunshine abundance.

Gremsa's stem is turned into the sun. (Oh James! What would you have shouted out some 30 years ago: "Widdershins beuy! Three turns wey the sun noo Mauri, to undo our hill witch's spell"). We are swallowed under the gaze of this immense blood red face.

Where have all the raucous whitmaa[92] gone - following fishing boats to distant shores now? Big nets mean fewer fish. Only mallimacks, tysties, bonxies and scarfs[93] left now to whitewash the rocks.

We tickle the very toes of the Auld Man with feathers and haul glistening cod over our gunnel, all dumb-faced and orange freckles. All sea by now is flat and cliffs magnified on this mirror. This yellow orb burns our heads pink in breathless air, shirts off now – can this be Orkney – 59 degrees North?

---

[91] The bung, the nile-hole allowing water to drain out when laid up.
[92] gulls
[93] Fulmars, guillemots, great skua and, indiscriminately, shags or cormorants

Three sailed spreet (sprit) rigged yoles racing at the Stromness Regatta c.1900. Ackroyd's large motor yacht Wolverine forms the start line. He paid cash prizes for yoles to race.

A zinc bath now full of cod is enough to accompany our winter chips, so we head deeper and leads hurl down for elusive ling. Ling is a slim, beautiful fish, all orange and green, firm and tasty flesh, as they tug-a-war with our fresh mackerel bellies. Keepers of cliffs and caves off the Auld Man. But we soon find the air stifling, blocked by huge cliffs, start our engine and troll inshore for golden lythe. A cool breeze at last.

Sunstruck rock faces glower right over us, with enormous boulders at their feet. Lythe seem to shelter among their shadows. More dried salt fish to rekindle summer on long, dark winter evenings.

The *m.v. Hamnavoe* races by with its urgent cargo of eager eyes. Our small yole can hardly be seen against the massive walls – a speck of humanity in this sea of fire today. At such a speed today do we miss small and precious things in life? The very people we come so far to meet?

As the 'Door of the Heel' opens out – the Kame's welcoming archway – we slip our last golden messenger from her blue threshold. This dark, jagged knife edge of rock cuts the deep sea in two. No more fish after we head into the Cuilag's dark shadowy ghosts. Too many shipwrecked fishermen lie here, warning the underworld of our intent.

The flood tide speeds our way into Stromness. So silent this powerful surge, twice a day, brings all the Atlantic to our sheltered doorstep. Hungry gulls greet us in a snowstorm of feather and screech. No waste from fish in this harbour.

A warm welcome of piers and gables, clustered under Bessie Millie's[94] gaze, which seems so far from the Auld Man's stony harshness. No human hand carved the cold walls out West.

Faces gather at the slip to haul our flattie and share our day. Cats purr with fishy dreams, while old folk's eyes glow with faint memories of their day at the Old Man.

Come and see the world, sail quietly by in a yole. Made in Orkney, for Orkney.

---

[94] Stromness's witch who lived on Brinkies Brae. For the sum of sixpence, Bessie would sell sailors a favourable wind. She would boil her kettle, and say her charms, and the sailor would be assured fair weather for sailing

The Gremsa showing how easily the three spreet (sprit) sail rig can be hauled down out of the way for fishing, off the massive cliffs on the Head of Hoy.

[In this next article, Maurice takes us on cruise No. 2, a trip from Stromness right round Hoy – a real adventure in a yole. It's not often that the wind and tide are right for such a trip, so truly this was one to be savoured.]

A SAIL ROOND HOY by Maurice Davidson

Mind on those couple of fine days last week? Just before the equinoctial gales swept in for five days from the North Sea. Time for a fish at the Old Man.

Blind grey fog held our yole prisoner early on Thursday morning, but the sun warrior slashed through and blue skies reigned all day.

Gremsa's three sails curved to the breeze as we cut a foaming white trail through the deep blue. Hoy Sound's conveyor belt whisked us out in the ebb, past three white sleeping sentinels to the jagged Kame. The Atlantic swell, heartbeat of the open sea, freed us from the land.

Suddenly our small open yole was shrouded in dark shadows under Hoy's huge battlements. Cold and eerie, then the Old Man tanned in welcome sunshine, with creel boats picking at his toes. Willack Sinclair[95] waves us on.

"We'll just have a look round Rora and see what's doing in the Firth". Breezy but flat. The flood was just starting to whisper against the warm wind in our face. We pushed out further into the Pentland Firth to get faster tide. Rackwick faded behind. Our wood and sail were a tiny speck in a huge sea, along the endless blood red buttress of Hoy's wild South side. A long way from anywhere.

We puttered our small outboard engine into life as the wind whistled along the cliffs, right in our faces. And the flood kept pushing us along, silent and strong.

The huge potbellied Old Man of Sneuk waved past, among wispy white trails from burns, as they tumbled over the edge. Rackwick Little lowered its head but held only a hard welcome. Then the glowing red Berry reared up in craig and gull before finally drawing out in low jagged spit - Torness.

We whisked past the small white sentinel here at nearly eight knots, close in, between rock and rough water. We turned this halfway corner and unfurled our sails from the masts again to fly along Hoy's southeast voes, calm but fast, in full flood, on the edge of a huge swirling tide eddy here.

Past Brims' welcome cottages and old lifeboat shed, another sentinel of the sea. Close in to Cantick Light, for a fish along its ragged cliffs, the flood urging us on past the quiet Kirkyard voe.

---

[95] Ex Stromness lifeboat skipper who went to the rescue of the Leicester City in 1953 in Hoy Sound

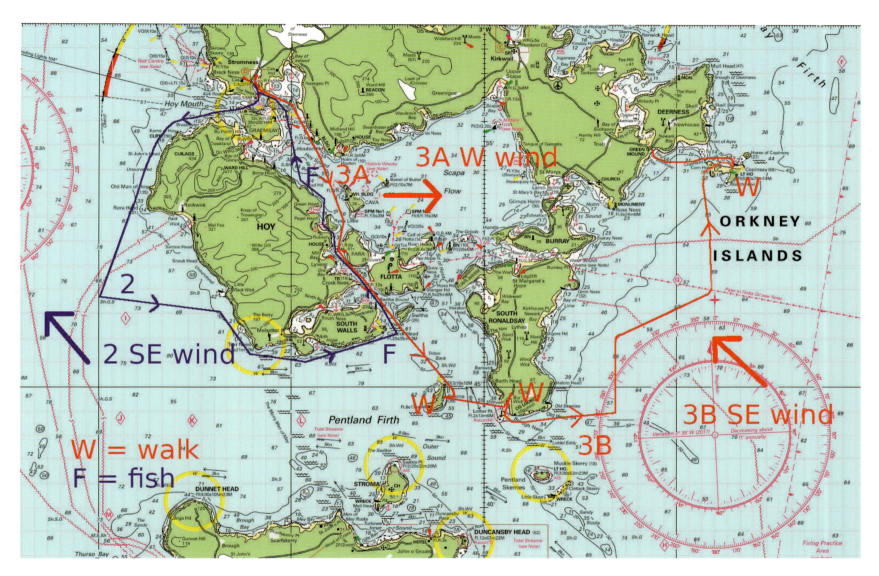

The routes of cruise Nos. 2 and 3 marked on. © Imray, Laurie, Norie and Wilson Ltd

Out of the surging ocean, sailing into the Flow (sounds like ow). Wind and tide urging us past stone sandcastles, guarding lovely Longhope.

A scatter of small islands and twisting sounds lead us to the Bring. We pull silvered fish up from under the cliffs of molten yellow cheese here.

Then the ebb set in again to pull Jan, Bill and me back to Stromness, our brown wings curving either side of the yole, like a gull in the breeze.

Thirty-six sea miles (40 miles) sailed round Hoy, in our 18-foot yole *Gremsa*, with the tide always behind us to quietly help us on. A lovely seven and a half hours basking in the sun and open sea.

Our strong tides and ocean surge don't allow such an enjoyable sail along these hard and lonely cliffs very often. Orkney's yoles have sailed here for hundreds of years until the last War, fishing or visiting neighbours. The tradition sails on.

2012 photo at Wick, of a newly built, traditional 18' decked Aberdeen yole Black Gold, built with oil wages, with dipping lugsail rig and fully decked.

2010. Bill, Jan and Maurice sailed their yole Gremsa past the Old Man of Hoy, into the Pentland Firth and caught the flood tide right round Hoy, fishing off Cantick and the Bring en route.

[Next up from Maurice is cruise No. 3, a lively tale of sailing down to Burwick at a rate of knots, and the following day of sailing up past Copinsay to Deerness under bare poles in a force 5-6 – far too lively for our taste. We gather also that the sleeping accommodation overnight on the Gremsa was less than comfortable....]

ROCK AND ROLL ROUND SOUTH RONALDSAY 2013 by Maurice Davidson

The weather has been unsettled this year. With a forecast of two or more fine days of westerlies, three OYA sailors made the most of this break. So late July saw Jan Andersen (68), Alfie Page (15) and Maurice Davidson (61) fly away on the flood from sunny Stromness. And what a journey we had on a warm force 4 west wind, in our 5-metre, open yole, the three sailed *Gremsa*.

Each takes turns at the helm and sails. Young Alfie has been sailing for over two years now, building up skills for his chosen career on the sea. Yoles change you.

We surge past the Flow's suntanned whale isles of Graemsay, Cava, Rysa, Fara and Flotta, on Hoy's gutsy hill breezes. Racing the red renewables barge at 6 knots, all the way to bustling Lyness – we leave no carbon trail.

One hour 40 minutes and lovely Longhope appears, then 20 minutes later we sail out past Switha into the open Atlantic swell of the Pentland Firth. A different heartbeat here stops Alfie's gob as the *Gremsa* cuts its white furrow up and down these long 3 metre hills. The swell flattens out in the strong flood and in 2 hours 45 minutes out, *Gremsa* curls round Swona's dancing tide race into the Haven. The only sheltered, yole-sized geo on a lonely shore.

With our fast sail, we have plenty of time for a 3-hour walk round this rough and fertile green isle, in the middle of a birling and swirling Pentland Firth. Old stone crofts slowly bow down to kiss the earth, as Rosies' owld kye[96] gawk at us alien intruders. Their house has been left as a time capsule, a reminder of how quickly life changes.

I can mind having tea here with the Rosies and James o' Garson, in the late 1960s. And sailing against their tall masted Orkney dinghy, the *Falcon*, towed over to the Longhope regattas by their big elliptical stern yole, the *Hood* – and all the crack at Whadiam's bar later. Now only silence.

The Annals, who own Swona, have done a good job of non-intervention conservation. Thanks for that. Then a huge red and white winged bird, the *m.v. Pentalina*, flies close by to our yole - with three big toots of her horn. Old and new live happily together.

We reach across to South Ronaldsay on the flood at nearly 11 knots! Wind and tide together. Then we rock and roll on and off the tip of a long underwater finger called the Creel, near Orkney Island Council's infamous 1980s Short Sea Route lego breakwater. A three hours' sail from Stromness.

---

[96] cattle

The Gremsa crew after their 2012 sail to Swona, with the elliptic sterned yole Hood built on Swona, left to fall in pieces at the head of the Haven when the island was abandoned in 1974.

Seems that a warning post on the Creel had rusted away, the local blacksmith Willie Mowatt having replaced it with a large brass pipe from a Skerries trawler, which was then stolen for scrap. Tough times, tough choices. Thanks to the lads on a creel dinghy, and Hamish Mowatt on his old lifeboat, for keeping a sea watch on us.

Burwick is a mainly shallow, rocky bay right on the southern tip of South Ronaldsay, now abandoned, with piles of concrete and rust, and a huge luxurious carpark! But it gives essential shelter for small boats and the John o' Groats ferry on this exposed headland.

Jan had to head off to the Balfour for a check-up, after one of our wooden spreets[97] slipped onto his nose while taking the sails down, at the floating ramp here. He was fine. This left Alfie and me to sleep on the yole, counting stars in a clear blue sky – with no midgies!

Next morning two of us set off with the first o' the flood, our small yole nipping along in smooth water, just inside rolling waves and overfalls of the Lother roost offshore. Small can be good. This is a high-energy headland and needs careful tidal timing and good weather to pass easily. Beware.

45 minutes later we head north up Orkney's east coast, where the wind and sea steadily build up to force 5 and 6 from the south east. Not the morning forecast of force 2 to 3 westerlies! Down to bare masts, using the outboard to control our steering after we lost the rear third of our poorly laminated rudder. We rock and roll in front of the one- to two-metre waves on our stern quarter as we surf down and along their faces - all 15 miles to Copinsay. In some large swaps, our yole flew along under some fairly sharp three-metre slopes like a Hawaiian boarder, frothy suds spraying in our faces, juddering with the noise of a train! Through two hours of this rollercoaster, now against a little flood, courtesy of the Stronsay Firth, our small double-ended yole proves dry and very seaworthy, if a little lively.

Squeezing inside the shallow Copinsay tide race, we use our iPhone charts to avoid the many rocks here and tie onto some creels in the bay sheltered by Black Holm. Alfie and I spend a couple of hours in complete relaxation, among caves and green slopes up to the spectacular cliff lighthouse. My auntie Clara Ritch was the last teacher for five kids here round World War II, living and teaching in the only farm. More school closures on our small isles, now all silent.

High water and we bounce across to one of the few slipways on Orkney's east shores at Newark Bay, Deerness. A welcome sight in the boisterous sea, but do watch oot for the breakwater at high water, it's under the water! Another sight we were glad to see was my lovely wife, towing our trailer and yole out of the waves. By the time we reached Stromness, there was no wind, the seas were calm and, of course, no one believed our wild eastern tale!

An eventful trip of 45 miles in 6 hours 15 minutes, averaging over 6 knots with a peedie[98] yole, with some good tides, good wind and help from some surfing waves.

And thanks to lots of friendly and helpful folk along the way. That's what is so enjoyable about sailing round our rocky shores.

---

[97] sprit - the long pole holding up the sail, diagonally to the mast

[98] small

2012 view of the Rosie's elliptic sterned yole Hood lying at the Haven, Swona where cattle have damaged her as they sheltered behind the hull in winter.

[Cruise No. 4 from Maurice takes us back to 2014 on a fascinating 40-mile trip from Tingwall, circumnavigating Eday, past spectacular scenery. Interesting, too, how an iPhone can put local tidal and rock knowledge at the fingertips of modern-day sailors.]

REFERENDUM SAILS ROUND EDAY by Maurice Davidson

Now the nights are draan[99] in, can you mind on those bright September days of 2014? Extraordinary events in Scotland, some more memorable than others!

Peedie[100] yoles sailing amongst our isles used to be ordinary, but no longer.

10am. Blue and white flags proudly flutter a Scottish welcome to Tingwall in Evie, still as sheltered a sandy bay as when used by our Viking friends a few years ago.

We haul our peedie longship cousin, a sharp ended 4.5-metre Orkney yole *Gremsa*, doon Eynhallow's slip. We hoist wer three red sails and slide away fae rock and kye[101].

The clutter and clatter of the referendum are left ahint[102] as we cut our white furrow past Cubbie Roo's massive stone castle on Wyre, turn left at the much objected-to fish farm site, and catch the ebb. We sail quietly by Egilsay's even more massive concrete ramparts, the Orkney Island Council pier sat on a huge shallow skerry.

Up on the hill lies the most beautiful building in Orkney, St Magnus' kirk with its slender round watchtower soaring into the sky. Wer[103] hidden gem.

Rousay's purple shoulders slip by, her low skirt of yellow barley having a busy trim today. We shoot through the narrow tidal twists of Longataing Sound. The last of the tide ebbs out for cheering waves of blue and white, as they hit shallow rocks.

Suddenly we are oot by Kili Holm, in wide open ocean, skipping over the long heartbeat of an Atlantic swell. The Waastree Furth (Westray Firth).

An hour later, past foaming white sheep forts of Rusk Holm, we find a low gap in the rock here at Fersness Sound. The flood urges us through this narrow gateway to the red cliffs of Eday and their birling tidal turbines. They work even better together here.

Faray's green stepping stones form a natural link from Westray to Eday, scattered with roofless crofts, flags all fallen down by now. A lonely stone slip lures us in near Dog Bones Point.

---

[99] drawing
[100] Little
[101] cattle
[102] behind
[103] Our

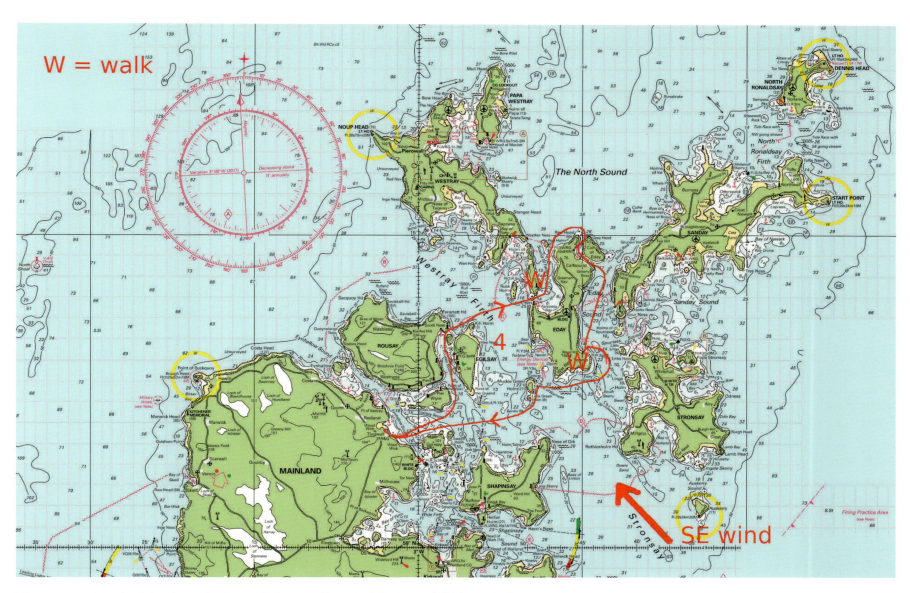

The route of cruise No. 4 marked on. © Imray, Laurie, Norie and Wilson Ltd

Strong winds swaap doon aff Eday's cliffs as we race round into Calf Sound at 7½ knots, past dramatic grey-haired and redhead sentries. The tide pushes us along this narrow, twisting river, past grassy crofts, demolition derbies (a local builder demolishing his almost finished home before our eyes) and wave splashed jetties. We avoid pirate Gow's last stand[104], wrecked between a rock and a hard place, under the glower of Eday's Scottish laird at Carrick House. Fea's saltire flies at half-mast today.

Our sail through history among these North Isles floods south, flying past a lonely London airport to the shelter of Backaland's stone quay. Ann's café/bar lies just above the pier, one of the cosiest in Orkney, with panoramic views over silage green slopes to Sanday's silver sands.

Then a visit to the gorgeous Veness of Eday, a stone croft, complete with coffee and coriander rock cakes, and off to see the Falls of Warness round the corner. With our fast sail we're a bit early to cross this tide strewn gateway of the Stronsay Firth. More rock cakes.

An hour later the noisy waves of blue and white subside, as the tide changes direction with the wind. Better together, to push us home in our peedie yole. We hoist our three redheads and sail on the southeast breeze over the last lumps of Warness for an hour. Good luck to our modern sea monsters, the yellow tidal submarines, birling in this turbulent flood. 6pm and no thanks to the red evening glow now in our sights, we slip west with the ebb, north o' the Galt and the Pap o' Gairsay as wer guide.

Soon we hear banging of tables and raucous singing, surely no a cooncil meeting or yet another referendum rally? – but no, it was Sweyn Asleifsson partying again in our imagination at his old holm.

Thanks to the friendly clam divers and lapster fishermen who helped us through the straits and narrows, and of coorse wer Veness of Eday and my brother Dennis for his company on the trip. Hids[105] the folk we meet on these isles sails that make them so enjoyable.

40 miles of twists and turns sailed over 6 ¾ hours, averaging 5 knots, with a little help from the moon. North Isles at their best, seen from the sea, sounds and heads up close, in a widen [106]three sailed yole.

And wer iPhone wis ferly handy too! It's vividly coloured GPS shows you hitting the tides and missing the rocks, jist. It's all on the app. Old and new, better together.

P.S. In my parents' generation, round Graemsay as well as other isles, yoles were ubiquitous. The only affordable way to fish, tak folk to the toon or carry peats and kye[107]. Journeys like the above were ordinary. We sail yoles round all wer isles, especially the more remote and tidal ones, to celebrate how extraordinary our forefathers' ordinary skill and knowledge was. When the extraordinary was ordinary, a 100 years ago.

---

[104] John Gow, captain of a notorious gang of pirates, was executed on 11th of August, 1729, for piracy
[105] It is
[106] wooden
[107] cattle

2014. Dennis and Maurice sail the Gremsa round Eday from Tingwall on the Orkney Mainland, and back.
They sailed with the strong tides here at all times, in lovely sunshine.

[Maurice's final contribution to this book serves as a fine excuse to include some wonderful photographs of yoles in the company of tall ships, on their visit to Stromness in 2011. He also captures some of the other Orkney yole activities that summer.]

2011, SMALL SHIPS AND TALL SHIPS by Maurice Davidson

OYA sailing started early in April this year and has gone right through all the rain till the end of September. We have had nearly six months at sea, up to seven yoles out sailing, twenty-one Thursday yole sail evenings, five regattas with OYA's *Lily* in the lead, two mornings' sailing with primary school children and a barbeque. In addition, we have enjoyed the visit of the Tall Ships.

2011 has not been outstanding for sunshine or settled weather. But it will be remembered for the sheer volume of sailing achieved, and the huge number of people who sailed on the sea in yoles. Over 413 visitors were taken out with more than 300 yole crew sailing trips.

In just three days of public sailing during the Tall Ships visit and the beginning of Stromness Shopping Week, over 230 visitors were taken out in Stromness' sheltered harbour. They came mainly to see this spectacular sailing scene up close, from our five small ships, but also to enjoy the views of the spectacular stone gables and piers. Yoles took more folk out sailing than the Tall Ships did! A dozen Norwegian crew members from the Tall Ships came out for a sail in our familiar-looking yoles. Hundreds of photos of our yoles were taken from the Tall Ships.

The stars of every year are always the enthusiastic Stromness P7 primary school children we take out for their first sail in May. 60 came this year, in just two yoles, over two busy mornings. The even better bit came later, when some of the children persuaded their mums and dads out for a sail at our barbeque. Their enthusiasm is addictive and they are our seed corn for the future. And it works. We now regularly have half a dozen young people learning to sail on Thursday evenings.

In addition to our weekly sailing and adding traditional colour to most regattas, yoles managed to sail out as far as the Old Man of Hoy for three sun-lashed days of fishing, catching cod and mackerel around his feet. Yes, there were some patches of settled weather this year, but even then, the wind blew up in the afternoons, to give a wet trip home.

The rebuilding of Flaws' Pier and Sail house finally started in July. Orkney Islands Council own this last old public stone pier in Stromness and the Orkney Yole Association now lease it as our traditional home base. Hard won grants funded the full restoration of this completely derelict property, along with a generous amount of volunteer labour given freely by OYA members.

Raymond Rendall and Bob Clouston have already completed a solid job in rebuilding the old crumbling stone pier front, just in time before recent southeast gales set in. The next job will be scaffolding of the old stone shed and its careful rejuvenation into our new/old sail store, boat store, social centre and meeting room. Flaws' pier will be kept open as Stromness's last old public stone pier, with everyone welcome to visit and photograph our yoles and open harbour views.

2011, small and tall pass each other at the entrance to Stromness harbour. The three spreet (sprit) sailed yole Gremsa reaches across the bows of a full sailed tall ship.

South isles yole Pansy in full flight, skippered by Kevin Kirkpatrick, at the abandoned Longhope Regatta 2007 due to F5-6 SW wind, yet see how sheltered the bay is.

[Sheena Taylor's next article introduces us to the Mowatt family of Burwick, South Ronaldsay, and their yoles and to the turbulent waters of the Pentland Firth in which they sail. This leads neatly on to the concluding article in the book, featuring Willie Mowatt in the Hope. We are delighted to include in the photographs a copy of a payment note for one of his catches sold direct to Billingsgate market in 1947, providing a fascinating glimpse of life back then.]

MOWATT FAMILY YOLES – *HOPE*, *STAR of BURWICK* and *VIVID* by Sheena Taylor

Of the many turbulent, tidal waters all around Orkney, the Pentland Firth is probably the most notorious for the challenges it presents. Close at hand to the south of South Ronaldsay are the Liddel Eddy and the confused waters round Old Head. Further south lie the Pentland Skerries, the treacherous whirlpool of The Swelkie (Old Norse, Svalga – The Swallower) and several exceptionally strong tidal currents, especially where the channel is at its narrowest at the eastern end of the Firth.

To the east of John o' Groats, the tidal race at Duncansby Head becomes the Boars of Duncansby running eastward on the flood.

As the ebb tide gathers strength travelling westwards, The Merry Men o' Mey begin their especial turmoil extending across the Firth from St John's Point to Tor Ness on the south of Hoy.

From Brims Ness the Merry Men can be seen kicking up their heels in the fastest section of their rapid dance in ever more boisterous reels, sets and turns sending spouts of water upwards in their frantic haste towards open water.

Between Cantick Head and Switha walls of water travelling in different directions jostle and shoulder their way to and fro there and in the Sound of Hoxa.

Ferry travellers can see for themselves how the waters all across the Firth swirl in smooth circular discs welling upwards, or descending into central depressions of varying sizes. Pilot notes for the Pentland Firth do not mince their words with the warning that small boats will be overpowered in strong winds and adverse tidal conditions.

It is straight into these waters that sailors like the Mowatts in the south of South Ronaldsay, Flotta and Hoy venture. Surely a place to know the state of the tide like the back of your hand, when the short spell of slack water will prevail and, also, to understand what the weather is likely to hold in store.

Willie Mowatt's son, Hamish, the present owner of the yole, *Hope*, provides some details of the boat's construction, the early days of his father skippering and of sailing with him.

Hope, 20 ft by 8 ft, was built in 1890 by Banks in Stroma. It is thought that the bow shape of *Hope* and other Stroma yoles was incorporated by the designer, Watson, into the design of the class of RNLI lifeboat bearing his name.

When Willie bought *Hope* from Doddy Gunn in John o' Groats in 1952, she was in poor condition. Willie rebuilt her with a new keel, stem and sternpost, replaced around half of the planks, as well as renewing the decking.

Willie Mowatt in stern and Steve Manson, in *Hope* at Pentland Skerries landing place, around 1970

Hope leaving John o' Groats

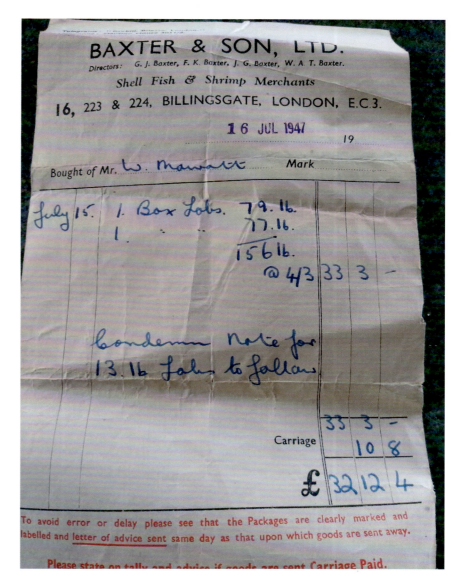

Lobster payment note

Willie registered *Hope* as K801 and fished for a few years. Steve Manson was crew for fourteen years, from 1956.

In 1958, Willie fitted a new 15-hp petrol Volvo Penta engine and gearbox, along with what was probably the first belt-driven capstan for hauling creels in Orkney. That work continued around Burwick and Pentland Skerries fishing lobsters. In the days before the founding of the Fishermen's Society in Orkney, Willie delivered his catch, and that of other fisherman in the area, to John o' Groats. The catch was transported to Thurso, and onwards for the twenty-four hour rail journey to the markets in Billingsgate.

Hamish recalls during his school days – or more accurately, he says, when he should have been at school – crewing in *Hope* while carrying fruit, vegetables, newspapers and many other goods between South Ronaldsay and John o' Groats, sometimes in more than one crossing per day in summer 1970, when the Dockers' strike disrupted the usual supply chain.

After Hamish bought a bigger 38-ft boat in 1976, *Hope* stood outside for the next forty years, while Willie and Hamish used the new boat. Willie also continued his trade as a blacksmith.

After Willie died, aged 91, in September 2016, Hamish decided to renovate *Hope*. The deck was in poor condition, but the hull was good, preserved by seventeen years of white lead paint. Hamish took the boat to Ian Richardson, Boatbuilder, in Stromness in January 2017, where a new deck was fitted exactly as it had been before.

Hamish burnt off all seventeen years of paint, repainted *Hope* and fitted a 15-hp Yammar diesel engine and gearbox in 2018. When he relaunched *Hope* in May 2019, he was pleased to see the boat "didn't even leak a drop!"

Star of Burwick preceded *Hope* as the family's fishing boat until *Hope*'s rebuild in the 1950s was complete. The *Star*, measuring 18 ft by 8 ft, was also built in Stroma sometime before 1890. She had belonged to Hamish's great-grandfather, John Mowatt, but it is not known whether that boat was new to him, nor whether she had a different name at one time.

In the late 1950s, Hamish's father had worked on a yole called *Vivid*, to fit a new stem and sternpost and a number of new boards for the owner Jimmy Dunnet in Windwick, South Ronaldsay. The boat was kept inside and was sold in Jimmy Dunnet's farm sale.

In 2018, Hamish bought *Vivid* - a Stroma yole measuring 18ft by 8ft and built in the early 1900s - and has since begun renovations.

Hope moored at Burwick when she was re-launched 2019.

Deck layout of the Hope, showing the traditional Stroma construction with half decks and covers, trying to keep the seas out, learning from nearby Moray Firth fishing yoles.

[The following article was compiled by Maurice Davidson in 2019 from notes of three vivid tellings over the years by Willie Mowatt of his adventure in 1959 in his smiddy in Burwick. At Willie's funeral in 2018, Maurice spoke to Geordie Rosie, the last man left from this trip. He said that no one would have made it through the Firth that day except for Willie; he knew all the tides around the Skerries, and really could handle a yole. Thorfinn Johnston has translated Willie's Orcadian dialect into English for us.]

WILLIE MOWATT'S STORMY SAIL TO THE SKERRIES[108] 14 June 1959

"I got caught oot wan day, beuy hid wis a right day, in the *Hope* ower there. Hid wis a fine morneen, as good as you get, and we went ower to Groats tae see me relations ower there. Efter sean eviry body I luked oot and hid had blown up a piece. A grand sailan breeze, so we aal went doon tae the shore and filled some secks wae sand fur ballast. Wey the wind ahint us wae wid go lik the devil today. Hid wis aal quiet at the pier, bit you kent by the wind in your hair that hid wis blowan herd fae the west ootside. My hell thir wis a lok o folk doon on the pier by the time wae finally got off in the efternoon. I think they aal kent hid wis gaan tae be a sight tae see under sail flyan ower tae Burrick.

Wae hoist up half the lugsail an flew oot o the pier on the flat sea. The further wae were aff the livelier hid got, grand speed, a real record o' a trip. Bit whan wae wer aboot half wey there everything got dark.

I got caught out one day. Boy it was quite a day, in the *Hope* over there. It was a fine morning, as good as you get, and we went over to Groats [109]to see my relations over there. After seeing everybody I looked out, and the wind had blown up a fair bit. A grand sailing breeze, so we all went down to the shore and filled some sacks with sand for ballast. With the wind behind us we would go like the devil today. It was all quiet at the pier, but you knew by the wind in your hair that it was blowing hard from the west outside. My hell, there was a lot of folk down on the pier by the time we finally got off in the afternoon. I think they all knew it was going to be a sight to see us, under sail flying over to Burwick[110].

We hoisted up half the lugsail and flew out of the pier on the flat sea. The further off we were, the livelier it got; grand speed – a real record of a trip. But when we were about halfway there, everything got dark.

---

[108] the Pentland Skerries, a group of small uninhabited islands in the Pentland Firth. The lighthouse on Muckle Skerry, now automated, was maintained by resident light keepers in the 1950s.
[109] John o' Groats, the most northerly village on the Scottish mainland.
[110] the southernmost district on the Orkney island of South Ronaldsay.

Willie Mowatt's large Stroma yole Hope taking eight passengers over to John o' Groats pier from Burwick, South Ronaldsay. Other Stroma yoles seen in the background.

I looked around and my heavens, whit a bloody sight, a big black bugger o a cloud aal the wey atween Dunnet and the Berry, an doon below hid the watter wis jist dancing white, an comman towards us at speed. You could hear the hissan o the spray bean blown aff the tops o the waves.

"Luk whits comman boys", an wae got the sail doon jist afore hid hit us with force. Jist a bang. You couldna hear a thing efter that wae aal the din o the win and watter. Wae jist hid tae run afore hid. The *Hope* is a big yole bit hid didna seem so big that day. The salt spray wis aal in your eyes and nose and you hid a job breathan in an seean whar ye were goan. I niver saa the lik o hid afore nor efter. White smoor. Jist the bare mast shaakan and the win screeman in the ropes, jist lik the telephone wires on the lan. Wae hid the engine gaan half speed only or you wid leap aff the lumps an run doon the face o hid. A sight to see if you could see hid. The gret big lumps o sea runnan under us as we raced rite afore hid. Jist as weel the flood wis in tae flatten hid a bit. Bit the seas wer high, and wae kept runnan rite in the middle o the sea or the crest wid spill aa ower us, ower the stern. Wae wer headdan to Norway and no stoppan. Wan man wis at the pump the whole time, pumpan fur life, the spray wis aa ower you. Seean whar you wer wis a problem, an whar ye wer gaan wis anither. Bit wae hid to handle the helm very carefully in the seas, hid wis a delicate job waae the big seas fae ahint you, hittan the stern right on. Liftan the boat bodily up then roaran under us as the spray wis gaen everywhere.

---

[111] Dunnet Head, the most northerly point on the Scottish mainland.
[112] a headland on the Orkney island of Hoy.

I looked round and, my heavens, what a bloody sight, a big black bugger of a cloud all the way between Dunnet[111] and the Berry[112], and down below it the water was just dancing white, and coming towards us at speed. You could hear the hissing of the spray being blown off the tops of the waves.

"Look what's coming, boys," and we got the sail down just before it hit us with force. Just a bang. You couldn't hear anything after that with all the din of the wind and the water. We just had to run before it. The *Hope* is a big yole, but it didn't seem so big that day. The salt spray was all in your eyes and nose, and you had a job breathing in and seeing where you were going. I never saw the like of it before or after. White spray blown off the wave tops. Just the bare mast shaking and the wind screaming in the ropes, just like the telephone wires on the land. We had the engine going at half speed only or you would leap off the lumps and run down the face of it. Just as well the flood was in to flatten it a bit. But the seas were high and we kept running right in the middle of the sea, or the crest would spill all over us, over the stern. We were heading to Norway and no stopping. One man was at the pump the whole time, pumping for life; the spray was all over you. Seeing where you were was a problem, and where you were going was another. But we had to handle the helm very carefully in the seas. It was a delicate job with the big seas behind you, hitting the stern right on, lifting the boat bodily up and roaring under us as the spray was going everywhere.

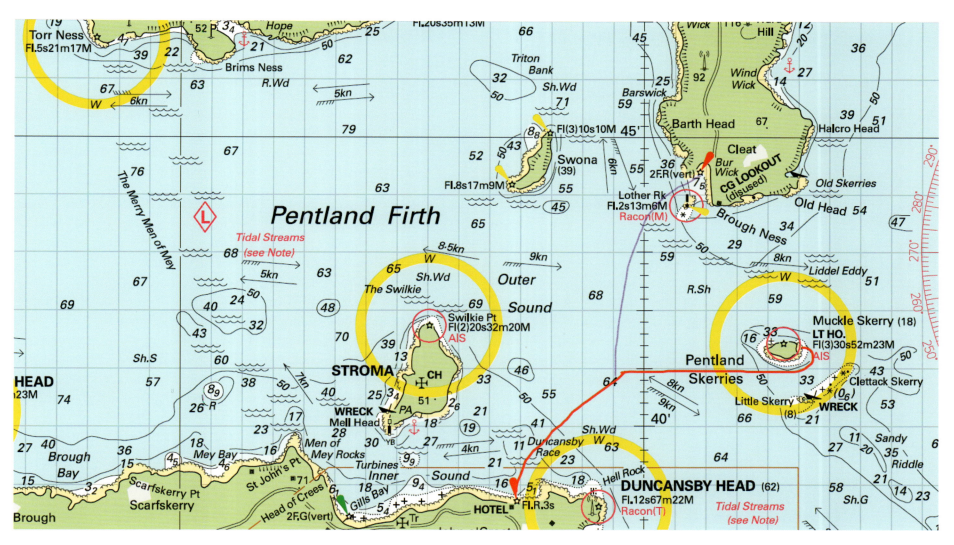

Willie Mowatt's journey – red line marks route taken; blue line marks planned route. © Imray, Laurie, Norie and Wilson Ltd

Bit the yole wis a good big yole and kept on top o the lumps as long as I could yank the tiller ower so the crest wid break either side o us. That wis the key. Bit me erm wis gettan tired. Bendan doon tae adjust the speed so we kept on the face o the sea an steeran wis tirean. Aal the bloody noise o the sea kept us going. Wae wir aa feart, and that kept us alive. And the *Hope*. I niver thout I'd see the huge lumps o sea rearan up ahint us, jist going the sam speed as us, ye thout ye could jist walk oot on top o hid if you slowed doon a bit.

Efter a while you got tae trust the boat completely as ye kent whit sheu wid do. An wae hid tae go through aal the worst o the sea in the Firth near the Skerries, lumps o watter coman up under you, knockan the boat aboot lik a footba an the watter started to come in ower the back end. I got a fright or two in among those white lumps, coman fae every side o the yole. I made it to the east landing, it wis like nite and day, flat and quiet efter aa the noise and spray in yur eyes, hurtan. Hid wis grand to get in there. Hid wis jist grand tae git a hand, an feel the lan under yur feet, steady. I kent damn fine the folk in Groats wid be thinkan wae wer gone in aal the win and I hid tae phone the coastguards from the lighthouse tae tell them wae wir aa rite, safe on the Skerries. The keepers couldna believe we hid made it through aal the white watter roond them.

But the yole was a good big yole and kept on top of the lumps as long as I could yank the tiller over so the crest would break either side of us. That was the key, but my arm was getting tired. Bending down to adjust the speed and steering so we kept in the face of the sea was tiring. All the bloody noise of the sea kept us going. We were all scared, and that kept us alive. And the *Hope*. I never thought I'd see the huge lumps of sea rearing up behind us, just going the same speed as us – you thought you could just walk out on top of it if you slowed down a bit.

After a while you got to trust the boat completely as you knew what she would do. And we had to go through all the worst of the sea in the Firth[113] near the Skerries, lumps of water coming up under you and knocking the boat about like a football, and the water started to come in over the back end. I got a fright or two in among those white lumps, coming from every side of the yole. I made it to the east landing. It was like night and day, flat and quiet after all the noise and spray in your eyes, hurting. It was grand to get in there. It was just grand to get a hand and feel the land under your feet, steady. I knew fine the folk in Groats would be thinking we were gone in all the wind, and I had to phone the coastguard from the lighthouse to tell them we were all right, safe on the Skerries. The keepers couldn't believe we had made it through all the white water around them.

---

[113] the Pentland Firth, a notoriously turbulent strait between the north coast of Scotland and the Orkney Islands. Its tides, channelled by land on both sides, are amongst the world's fastest, reaching up to 30 kilometres per hour.

Left to right: Willie Mowatt, Alan Budge, George (Geordie) Rosie, 2 lighthouse keepers, Tom Budge (Alan's older brother), another lighthouse keeper. Photograph provided by Hamish Mowatt and taken by Sandy Scarth

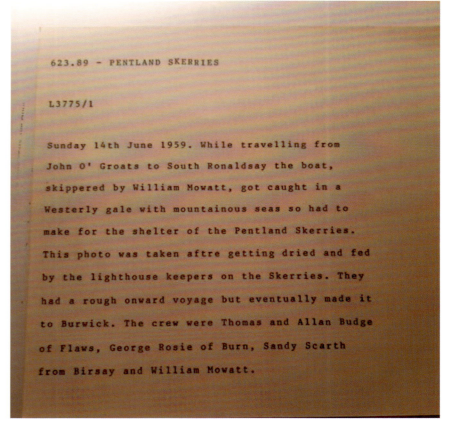

Contemporaneous record, provided by Hamish Mowatt

When we opened ther door, we walked into the keepers room, aal warm an calm wae the win screeman around wer lugs. Ye wid hiv thout they hid seen a ghost, they wir stunned an stared at us, dreepan weet on thir floor, eyes sweean wae the salt. "Where the hell hiv you come fae?" "Groats". I asked the principal "Could you be good enough to phone Duncansby light an tell the lifeboat we wir aarite, and not to send the lifeboat oot." "That's a hell o a wind oot there tae be on the watter" he replied wae a mug o tea fur us aa, sittan on boxes on the floor. "Yes, bit I got caught oot wae a change o weather."

Dan Kirkpatrick wis ready to launch the Longhope lifeboat when he got a call fae the lighthouse an he jist couldna believe we hid made it through aal that sea, 75 mph, I jist said "hid wis a damn sight more than that at the Skerries, jist screemen at us."

The folk wae me hid a camera bit wir feart to use it, hid wid hiv been a sight as they wer facean hid aal, mountains o seas an aal the frothy suds roond the yole as the lumps roared by. Dan didna ken hoo wae cam through hid aal. In a peedie open yole. Bit I had complete confidence in the *Hope*, she lifted to aal the lumps from every direction near the Skerries, throwan aboot lik a horse, bit dry. Wae wir aal bruised for days efter wae the bangan aboot wae hid. I don't ken how wae cam through hid aal, an that's the truth."

When we opened their door, we walked into the keeper's room all calm and warm, with the wind screaming around our ears. You'd have thought they'd seen a ghost; they were stunned and stared at us, dripping wet on their floor, eyes stinging with the salt. "Where the hell have you come from?" "Groats." I asked the principal, "Would you be good enough to phone Duncansby[114] light and tell the lifeboat we were all right, and not to send the lifeboat out." "That's a hell of a wind out there to be on the water," he replied with a mug of tea for us all, sitting on boxes on the floor. "Yes, but I got caught out with a change of weather.

Dan Kirkpatrick[115] was ready to launch the Longhope lifeboat when he got the call from the lighthouse, and he just couldn't believe we had made it through all that sea, and 75mph winds. I just said, "It was a damn sight more than that at the Skerries, just screaming at us."

The folk with me had a camera but were scared to use it. It would have been a sight as they were facing it all, mountains of seas and all the frothy suds around the yole as the lumps roared by. Dan didn't know how we came through it all, in a little open yole. But I had complete confidence in the *Hope*. She lifted to all the lumps in every direction near the Skerries, throwing about like a horse, but dry. We were all bruised for days afterwards, with the banging about that we had. I don't know how we came through it all, and that's the truth."

---

[114] Duncansby Head, a few miles to the east of 'Groats', where the north and east coasts of the Scottish mainland meet, and where a lighthouse is situated.
[115] legendary coxswain of the Longhope (Hoy) lifeboat, which was involved in many heroic exploits owing to its proximity to the Firth. Dan was Coxswain from 1954-1969, saving many lives during that time, and was awarded two silver medals by the RNLI.

Stroma yole Hope in 2000 at South Ronaldsay built by Banks in 1895 for fishing cod in the Firth and originally a three sailed spreet yole. Owned by the late Willie Mowatt.

Appendix

DEVELOPMENT OF YOLES TO THE SOUTH AND WEST OF ORKNEY by Maurice Davidson

Yoles are found in all Viking areas of Britain. They tend to look more like Orkney yoles, built to carry more load for more people down south. Yet they are still lightly built to launch and haul up beaches. From Wick to the Thames estuary, these open, sharp-ended, clinker boats are universally called yawls, showing the southern influence. The Yorkshire yawl rigged lug sails, easier to work on larger yoles, with two masts widely spaced for more work space. Lugsail became the name for the boat as well as for the sail rig.[xliv]

By the late 1700s and early 1800s, inshore fishing was flourishing, with high prices, as the impact of the Napoleonic Wars closed southern waters. Later, fish were needed to provide the new industrial city workers down south with cheap protein. 5.5-metre yoles, 18 feet over ends or 13 feet of keel, 2.2 metres wide yet with only 0.6 metres draft aft, built with ten or eleven strakes, became the standard open boat for four or six men to fish safely, a few miles offshore, and haul up a beach each night.

Moray Firth scaffies were yoles built with a vertical curved stem, to give a fuller bow and had a Yorkshire lug sail rig for simplicity, with only one short yard on one standing mast. This meant there was not much to get in the way of fishing and they were easy to handle. For mainland Scottish boats had only to sail out a few miles, then back again. So, they had an easier time, with no islands to tack around or tides to cross. These open, clinker yoles reached lengths of ten metres or more in the 1870s before disasters at sea brought in larger decked scaffies for safety.[xliv]

Aberdeen yoles had a vertical stem and a very sloped or raked stern post, to elongate the yole as much as possible, and were cheaper to build with less wood. The longer the yole, the faster it goes, and the more fish it can carry. They were harder to build, but there were full-time boat builders on these well populated coasts.

Further south, Fife coast open yoles, still only 13 feet of keel for hauling up a beach, were influenced by English fishers, with vertical stems and more vertical sternposts. Much slimmer ends on these ***Fifie yoles*** gave more speed in light winds and seas there; but meant that they were less buoyant.[xliv]

Zulu skiffs were a smaller, clinker mixture of Fifie bows and scaffie sterns, which led to the shape of the most popular and safer, large 15- to 20-metre decked carvel herring drifters of the late 1880s. All these large boats came about only after several disasters at sea with large open yoles, which led to the building of many stone harbours and other changes following the Government's Washington Report in 1849.[xliv]

Yorkshire fishermen built similar yawls but also developed flatter bottoms with internal keels, as they had few good harbours and used rivers to beach the boats on each night. Latterly, the sides became very rounded to help pull nets over, and developed into cobles with square transoms.

The very slim **Thames yawls and skiffs** were double-ended, light clinker yoles for fishing and piloting of larger ships up river. They were built for speed, to cover long distances, reach shipping first, and get the job before the competition. These yawls became longer to get more speed, and used a two-mast yawl rig with sprit sails to catch more wind. You can still see these very fast yawls, up to ten metres long, in regattas on the South Coast. They were 2 to 2.5 metres wide, with huge crews of ten for ballast, or for rowing in the lighter winds of their estuaries.[xliv]

Vikings also headed south down the west coast of Scotland and left behind their yoles with the Gaels, to develop fishing. More recent Orkney yoles bought by local landowners, initially in Stornoway, helped to develop cod fishing in the 1770s, after the lairds had cleared thousands of people from their lands.

Later, in the 1840s, after the extreme poverty of the potato famines, thousands left again, this time for a better life in Australia or Canada. So, the lairds again imported Orkney yoles, to get more money into their pockets, and maybe some food for their hungry crofters.

Sgoths, as yoles are called in Gaelic, were built locally and in Ullapool, for the cod cash market.

Sgoths Niseach became larger, up to eight metres long with fine, higher bows to survive beach launching in the surf at Niss, or Ness, which was the nearest landing to the Butt of Lewis and to give access to deep gretline[116] fishing grounds to the west. Sterns became rounder and fatter, using very wide strakes, with the best larch from the Highlands. This helped to land sgoths, stern on to seas, without swamping on steep beaches. These larger open sgoths were even used for herring nets, in their new harbour after 1840, but this proved too dangerous. Sgoth crews, and a lack of jobs, led to the Western Isles providing a major source of merchant seamen for the British Empire.[xxxviii]

Sgoths, and **Grimsay yoles** on the Monach Isles to the southwest of Uist, were powered by a dipping lugsail. This was one tall, standing mast on six-metre boats and two on the larger eight-metre sgoths. They were awkward to tack, cheap and simple but usable, as they mainly sailed out to sea and back again. Huge stresses on the hull from larger masts, to get faster speeds and go further out for larger fish, burst many hulls. Huge baulks of wiring, fore and aft stringers, line the mast thafts (thwarts) to spread these loads and avoid leaks, as seen on the two remaining sgoths.

Yoles also made it to Ireland, imported by Viking traders to their largest slave market in Dublin, founded in 814A.D.. These yoles were still employed by lairds up until World War II on the more isolated Aran islands, to provide jobs and cash from fishing.

Drontheim yawls, once common across the whole of the north coast of Ireland, were local variants of Trondheim yoles, still imported in the 1700s from Norway, and through the Caledonian canal in the 1850s. These yawls are typical yoles, double ended, sharp to cut the surf, five to eight metres long yet only two metres in beam as they

---

[116] These are long fixed lines of baited hooks set and hauled after three to six hours

had little tide to cross. They were clinker built but with vertical stems and stern posts for rowing speed. Larch strakes were attached to fitted oak frames, as in sgoths and our Orkney yoles. One or two simple, cheap dipping lugsails were used to power the heavy-laden fishing boats back to their home port.[xlv]

People in Ireland were poor after the potato famine and they (or their lairds) built their yoles lightly to save money. Small keels had to be replaced every four years after rough beach landings, with sand keel wings to avoid rebates and keep building cheaper. Short boards were used to make the curves and save money and home-made copper roves made from cut sheet all gave these yoles, and their crews, a short, wet life.

Sprit sails, as used on small ships' boats in the Royal Navy for extra speed in tacking, were used here to give a larger open work area between two standing masts. Nowadays, they are used to give easier tacking in regattas.

Neiss (Ness) 21 foot Sgoth from Lewis, Western Isles running in front of a good Easterly breeze all the way from Stromness to Stornaway overnight in 22 hours, with her large lugsail.

Register of Yoles in seaworthy condition – this is given in good faith, at the time of publication. However, no responsibility or liability can be assumed or implied for errors, inaccuracies, or change of circumstance. And despite the collators' best efforts, there may yet be omissions. Please contact the OYA with any updates or corrections. Thanks to Ron Bulmer, John Budge, Caroline Butterfield, Ian Richardson, Sheena Taylor and Captain Willie Tulloch for their help in its compilation.

Boat	Date built	Builder	LOA	Where kept	Notes
Hope	1890	Banks of Stroma	21'	South Ronaldsay	A Stroma yole (beam 8ft). Originally WK529. Bought by Willie Mowat in 1952, becoming K801. His son, Hamish, had the boat refurbished by Ian Richardson in 2017, and she went back in the water in 2019 with a new engine.
Sumato	1893	John Duncan of South Ronaldsay	21'	Stromness	First registered for fishing as K494 *Jeanette*. Name changed to *Sumato* in 1938 when re-registered for fishing as K494.
Irene	1908		16'8"	Kirkwall	
Family Pride	1910	Built Flotta	18'	Brims	Fishing Register as K619, indicates built Flotta in 1913. Built for Tom Kirkpatrick, great grandfather of current owner. Originally named *Family's Pride* first registered for fishing (K295)
Emma	1912	James Nicolson, Flotta	18'	Brims	K629. Built on Flotta, now at Brims. Restored by John A Mowat
Mohican	1912	Built Flotta	18'	Longhope	K691 record of first registration for fishing by James Thomson, Flotta, in 1919, indicates she was built in 1912. Built for Dr Hay, the doctor on Flotta, for recreational use. Dr Hay may have worked with the Mohican tribes, hence name. The boat went to Stromness, became *Irene*. Regained her original name on return to Longhope.
Waterwitch	1923	Edward (Ned) Jamieson, Hackness	18' 6"	Stromness	Originally K314 *Azalea*. Name changed when relaunched by Rod Daniel following a rebuild in 2012 at the IBTC, Lowestoft.
Clearway	1965		19'	Kirkwall	
Grebe	1974	Sinclair, Burray	18'	Hoy	
yole	1985	Ian B Richardson	20'	Uig, Lewis	Built as a sheep boat.
Helga	1996	Ian B Richardson	18'	Stromness	Built on lines taken from *Emma*.
Halle	1997	Ian B Richardson	16' 6"	Leith	
Frances	1998	Ian B Richardson	17'	Flotta	
Gremsa	1999	Len Wilson, Kirkwall	18'	Stromness	Built on lines taken from *Family Pride*.
Lotte	2001	Ian B Richardson	16'6"	Longhope	Formally *Philabin*. Came back to Orkney from Ireland

Boat	Date built	Builder	LOA	Where kept	Notes
Eve	2006	Ian B Richardson	18'	Kent	Elliptic stern
Lily	2008	Ian B Richardson	18'	Stromness	Built for Orkney Yole Association
Wonne	2011	Ian B Richardson	18'	Holland	Elliptic stern
Lady Hamilton	2013	Ian B Richardson	18'	France	Elliptic stern
Solwen	2014	Ian B Richardson	18'	Stromness	
unnamed	2016	Ian B Richardson	18'	Stromness	
Swansong	2019	Ian B Richardson	19'	Norfolk	Elliptic stern
Francis			14' 9"	Westray	Westray yole
Rosebud				Holm	Motorised yole, restored and used as safety boat by Holm Sailing Club
Bonnie Lass			18' 1"		Sold by Ian Richardson.
Ivy				Longhope	Tan sprit sails.
Others which were seaworthy recently or shortly to be restored:					
Lizzie ll	2008	Andrew and Richard Wilson (father and son), Kirkwall	14.6'	In storage, Holm	This is a replica of a boat built by Thomas Omand, Burness, Sanday, in the 1870s. The original boat was owned at one time by Andrew's father, and restored by the Wilsons in 2003, before being gifted to Orkney Islands Council, and is now in Lyness Museum. Lizzie II (the replica) was sold by the Wilsons in 2017 and is currently in store in Holm. Quite a small North Isles yole at 14'6" in length and 6'2" beam.
Bee	1905	Duncans of Burray	20'	Westray	A South Isles yole. Beam 7ft 6 in. K70. Moved to Westray in 1931 when acquired by Hugh Costie. She remains in the family and Geordie Costie was still fishing with her in 2019.
Irene	1908	Believed to be by Scott of Stumpo, Sanday.	16' 2"	In storage, Kirkwall	Small North Isles yole? Beam 6.7ft. K156/K664 In very good condition when viewed in the recent past by Orkney Historic Boat Society (OHBS). Work done in recent years by Smith Foubister. Now with Robbie Drever, who plans to prepare her for going back in the water.
Doris	c1930	John Renton Baikie, Stromness	17' 8"	In storage, Stromness	K188. Beam 7ft. Decking and gunwales restored by Ian Richardson, 2006? Now in ownership of OHBS. In store in Stromness.
Sea Astrid	1949	William Ritch, Deerness	20' 2'	In storage, Deerness	K92. Beam 7.9ft. Recently returned to Orkney and restoration taken on by Sydney Foubister and friends in Deerness, who plan to fully restore her. Returning to seaworthy condition?
Kathleen			13'	Kirkwall	

Glossary

Boat parts	
apron	Timbers which are attached on the inside of the stem or stern to provide 'landings' to which the planks are attached fore and aft.
breasthook (hunnyspot)	A knee used to reinforce the junction between the gunwales or sheerline at both the stem and stern of the boat.
clenching (riveting)	The use of a convex shaped washer which is clenched (fastened) around a copper nail to form a rivet.
hog	A timber which is attached on top of the keel to provide a 'landing' to which the garboard planks are attached.
knee	A curved piece of **wood used to** reinforce major junctions, for example, between the keel and the stem or stern of the boat.
mould	A pattern of frames temporarily attached to the hog in order to shape the planks to the required design of the boat.
plank (strake)	A board used in forming the skin of the hull.
rabbet (rebate)	Generally, the term refers to the grooves cut into the sides of the keel, stem, and sternpost, into which the garboards and hooding ends of the outer planking are seated.
rove	A convex copper washer used in clenching (fastening) copper nails.
stringer	A fore and aft timber fixed to the inside surfaces of the hull skin to provide strength and stiffness.
scarf	A long, tapered joint used to connect 2 planks together, while retaining much of the strength of a solid plank.

timmer (rib)	A thin transverse member composed of one or several pieces, that stiffens the skin of a hull.
Birds and Fish	
bonxie	the Great Skua
cuithe	coal fish
lapster	lobster
lythe	[also: lithe] pollack
mallimack	fulmar petrel
partans	edible brown crabs
scarf	applied to both shags and cormorant
sillock	coal fish
tystie	guillemot
whitmaa	gull, of any variety. The Orcadian version of 'seagull'.
Vessels	
m.v. Hamnavoe	SERCO Northlink's ferry that links Orkney to Scotland, from Stromness to Scrabster
Leicester City	a fishing vessel that came to grief on Hoy's northern shore
m.v. Pentalina	operated by Pentland Ferries, the m.v.'Pentalina' plied between St Margaret's Hope and Gills Bay.
Stratheliot	a fishing vessel that came to grief on Hoy's northern shore
	Geography
Cuilags	Orkney's second-highest hill range
Falls of Warness	a test site for the renewable industry – especially for tidal energy.
Flaas'	Flaws' Pier. Nestles adjacent to Stromness Museum
Kame	Hilltop. Kame o' Hoy – a prominent headland
London Airport	the airfield on Eday
sooth	south

Waastree Furth	Westray Firth
Orcadian Dialect	
aal	all
ahint	behind
auld	old
beuy	originates from Old Norse - búi – dweller, inhabitant, neighbour. It applied to both genders, but is now more frequently used for men, possibly because of confusion with 'boy'
birling	spinning
bowspreet	bowsprit
cooncil	council
coorse	course
creel	lobsterpot
dooked	ducked
draan	drawing
efter	after
ferly	fairly
geo	a rocky inlet
gizened	dried up; especially when barrel staves open up.
gret lines	long lines of baited hooks
herd	hard
hids	it is
holm	small island
jist	just
keps aff	caps off
ken, kent	know, knew
kye	cows; one of the very few remnants from the now lost Norn language
lug	ear
luk	look
mind on	remember
mooth	mouth
nile	the plug used to drain water in boats
noo	now
oot	out
ower	over
raffles	a mess, tangle
roond	round
roost	tide – Orkney's tides are notoriously quick.
peedie	small
seex	six
Simmer Dim	twilight around midnight in Orkney, when the sun barely sets, in midsummer
sook	suck
speer	look closely at
spik	speak
spreet	sprit [long wooden pole keeping the sail up at an angle off the mast]
Swap or swap	a gust of wind
tak	take
tatties	potatoes
thaft	thwart or seat
timmers	frames or planks
toon	town i.e. Kirkwall or Stromness
voe	a bay or inlet to the sea
wark	work
weel	well
wer	our – not dissimilar to the Geordie 'wor'.
quill	a 3.5 – 4.5 metre slim yole with curved ends
wid	would
widdershins	anticlockwise
widen	wooden
wis	was

Further reading

Reference Books on Yoles

Fenton A *The Northern Isles: Orkney and Shetland* John Donald Publishers Ltd 1978.

Firth H N *The People of Orkney: Aspects of Orkney* The Orkney Press Ltd 1986.

Fjellsson S *Spriseglet* (Sprit boats of Norway) 2002 pamphlet.

Greenhill B and Mannering J *Inshore Craft: Traditional Working Vessels of the British Isles* 1997

Groat W *The Sea Under My Counter* 1980.

Harcus S *Tight Sheets – Traditions and Tales* Westray Sailing Club 2006.

Harcus S *Skeegersome* Westray Sailing Club/Westray Heritage Trust 2016.

Houston A *Lest we forget: The Parish of Canisbay* Canisbay Parish Church 1996.

Indruszewski G *Origin of the Clinker Hull Construction* Roskilde Uni. www.Academia.edu 2018.

Low G *Low's History of Orkney* (1780s) Orcadian Ltd Revised edition 2001.

McKee E *Working Boats of Britain: Their Shape and Purpose* Conway Maritime Press 1983.

MacPolin D *The Drontheim: Forgotten Sailing Boat of the North Irish Coast* Dublin 1992.

March E J *Inshore Craft of Great Britain* David & Charles 1970.

Miller J *A Wild and Open Sea: The Story of the Pentland Firth* The Orkney Press 1994.

Nyheim H S *Norce Boat Dictionary (of all North lands)* 2007 pamphlet *Foreningen Allmogebatar Trabiten* 2004 Bassholmen, Sweden.

Omand D *The Orkney Book* Birlinn Ltd 2003.

Orkneyinga Saga: The History of the Earls of Orkney, translated by Palsson H and Edwards P. Penguin 1981.

Osler A G *The Shetland Boat: South Mainland and Fair Isle* Trustees of the National Maritime Museum 1983.

Sandison C *The Sixareen and her racing descendants* Shetland Times Ltd 2005.

Schei L V & Moberg G *The Orkney Story* Harper Collins 1985.

Thompson W P L *Orkney Crofters in Crisis* Orcadian Ltd 2013.

Tinch D *Shoal and Sheaf: Orkney's Pictorial Heritage* Colourpoint Creative Ltd 1988.

Towsey K *Orkney and the Sea: an oral history* Orkney Islands Council 2002.

Walker A *Stroma Yoles: their construction and development* Orcadian Ltd 2004.

Wilson B and Allardyce K *Sea Haven: Stromness in the Orkney Islands* The Orkney Press 1992.

Photograph Credits

Thank you to all photographers and owners of photographs that have allowed us to use their work in this book, and this book only. Copyright of all photographs used in this book belong to the photographers or owners of the photographs, and their written approval must be obtained before any use can proceed. Photographs integral to articles are credited directly by their authors.

PHOTOGRAPHER/OWNER	PHOTOGRAPH PAGE
Dave Bowdler	178, 182
Ron Bulmer	115a
Dennis Davidson	10, 11, 42, 56, 134, 143, 176, 192, 222.
Jessie Davidson	89, 108
Maurice Davidson	cover, v b, viii, 2, 3, 6, 12, 20, 28, 30, 38, 44, 46, 48, 50, 52, 53, 62, 68, 69, 74, 80, 93, 94, 96, 98, 99, 110, 115b, 116, 117, 118, 120, 122, 126, 128, 130a, 130b, 132, 135, 137, 138, 142, 146a, 148, 154, 156, 158, 159, 160, 161, 180, 181b, 196, 199, 200, 202, 204, 208, 214b, 225.
A Drever	162
Frantic Films	90
S Harcus	150
Bill Hercus	112
Thorfinn Johnston	187
Michael McLaughlin	114, 210a
John A Mowatt	184, 186a
Hamish Mowatt	212a, 212b, 212c, 214a, 216
Ian Montgomery	v a, 172
Isobel Norquoy	186b
Orkney Library and Archive	iii, vii, ix, 4, 18, 22, 26, 32, 34, 54, 67, 76, 82, 84, 86, 87, 88, 100, 102, 104, 106, 139, 140, 144, 152, 190, 194.
Stromness Museum/Estate of Stanley Cursiter	24
Peter Swanson	70
Craig Taylor	78
Sheena Taylor	14, 16
George Thorpe	124
Trabiten	8
Willie Watters	36a, 36b, 146b, 174a, 188, 210b
Wick Heritage Centre	40, 72

References

[i] Orkneyinga Saga by Snorrie (1230s)
[ii] Inshore Craft of Great Britain by Edgar March (1970)
[iii] The Shetland Boat by Adrian Osler (1983)
[iv] See ii and iii
[v] Vikings by Neil Oliver, book in conjunction with BBC4 (2013)
[vi] Origin Of The Clinker Hull Construction, Roskilde Uni. by George Indruszewski (2010)
[vii] Pamphlet NORCE Boat Dictionary (2007)
[viii] *The Viking*, ed, Tre Trycare, C.A Watts and Co Ltd. London, 1966
[ix] The Norse Waterways of West Mainland Orkney, Scotland by Martin Bates, Richard Bates, Barbara Crawford and Alexandra Sanmark
[x] Marwick, Hugh, *Proceedings of the Orkney Antiquarian Society*, 1926
[xi] NRS (National Records of Scotland), E504/26/6 & 7 Kirkwall Customs Accounts, 1781-1796
[xii] OA (Orkney Archive), D2/34/13
[xiii] NRS, CS228/IJ/2/20
[xiv] Knox J, *A Tour through the Highlands of Scotland and the Hebride Isles in 1786*
[xv] OA, D2/41/9
[xvi] Old Statistical Account (OSA), Birsay & Harray
[xvii] OSA, Stromness
[xviii] Stromness census 1821; *Kirkyards of Stromness and Graemsay*, 1999 and other documents
[xix] Traill, W, Rev, *Vindication of Orkney*, 1823
[xx] Omond, J, *Model of the safest and handiest Sailing Fishing-boat, as to hull, sails, spars and rig*, 1883
[xxi] OA, D24/4/190, Melsetter Estate Accounts, 1794
[xxii] OSA, Walls and Flotta, c.1794
[xxiii] Fereday, R P (editor), *The Autobiography of Samuel Laing of Papdale 1780-1868*.
[xxiv] Tudor, John, *The Orkneys and Shetland; their past and present state*, 1883
[xxv] OA, D2/5
[xxvi] Davidson, Frank, pers com (personal comment)
[xxvii] Davidson, Frank & Wilson, James, pers com
[xxviii] Tudor, John, *The Orkneys and Shetland; their past and present state*, 1883
[xxix] SM (Stromness Museum), Baikie Accounts Ledger (boatbuilder); Wilson, James & Davidson, Frank, pers com
[xxx] The Orkney Book by Donald Omand (2003)
[xxxi] Inshore Craft of Great Britain by Edgar March (1970)
[xxxii] The Shetland Boat by Adrian Osler (1983)
[xxxiii] Inshore Craft of Great Britain by Edgar March (1970) and The Orkney Book by Donald Omand (2003)
[xxxiv] The Northern Isles by Fenton (1978)
[xxxv] Stroma Yoles by Alastair Walker (2004)
[xxxvi] The Shetland Boat by Adrian Osler (1983) and The Sixareen by Charles Sandison (2005)
[xxxvii] Foreningen Allmogebatar Trabiten (2004), Bassholmen, Sweden
[xxxviii] Working Boats of Britain by McKee (1983)
[xxxix] The Parish of Canisbay by Anne Houston (1996)
[xl] Working Boats of Britain by McKee (1983) and Inshore Craft by Basil Greenhill and Julian Mannering (1997)
[xli] The Sixareen by Charles Sandison (2005)
[xlii] Orkney Crofters in Crisis by William P L Thompson
[xliii] Orcadian newspaper reports
[xliv] Inshore Craft by Basil Greenhill and Julian Mannering (1997)
[xlv] The Drontheim by Donal MacPolin (1992)